More Than A Story

DANI TIETJEN

HENRY GRAF

Abby -
Proud to Know
& work with
you -
Dani T

Mightier Press - Fort Wayne, Indiana
www.MightierPress.com

More Than A Story

Copyright © 2013 Mightier Press

ISBN: 978-0-9910243-7-7

Published by Mightier Press

Box 5312

Fort Wayne, Indiana 46895

www.MightierPress.com

Cover concept by Katrina Hannemann, Brett Dorrian, Dani Tietjen, and Henry Graf.

Photography by Katrina Hannemann with Studio Laguna Photography www.stulagu.com.

Hair and Makeup by Brett Dorrian with Brett Dorrian Artistry Studio www.brettdorrian.com.

Graphic Design and Layout by Paul Tietjen.

Print Production by Vision Van Gogh www.visionvangogh.com.

Photo's taken at Blue Horse Farm in New Richmond, Wisconsin www.bluehorsefarm.com.

IndieGoGo campaign video by Todd Reynolds

This book is dedicated to

Paul,

Never have I met a man who loves

as deeply and selflessly as you.

Thank you for the sacrifices you made for this project;

just add it to my tab.

- Dani

Tricia,

Though I fill a book,

I'm still at a loss

for words cannot begin express

the depth of my love for you.

- Henry

Table of content

It takes a village...

People say it takes a village to raise children. They also say writing a book is like having a child. Well, no project that is worth doing is easy or can be done alone, and we have been incredibly blessed by an amazing village of people who have rallied behind us. Their names need recognizing because this project wouldn't exist without them.

Katrina Hannemann and Brett Dorrian thank you so much for the time, energy, and countless conversations to create a book cover that is a work of art in its own right. It is always such a pleasure to work with two strong women who are dedicated to high quality.

Guy Mahmarian you gave incredible advice and helped direct us in the right direction. We are indebted to you for the quality of professionalism that you brought to this project.

Paul Tietjen your artistic counsel, direction and dedication made this plain book beautiful. Thank you for the hours you poured into turning into this final masterpiece.

Chad Amour, Ben Bruns, Inga Decker, Tricia Graf, Nancy Holden, Chad Speller, Kim Waller, and Cassie Woodard you gave up hours of your time to pour over these words on a tight deadline to take a good book and make it great. Thank you for your sacrifice in this project and your belief in us. This book is better because of you.

Laura Cichon what a beautiful surprise gift you are. Thank you for taking a final read to make sure the words were ready for the reader.

Thank you to Karla at Blue Horse Farm for creating an Art Farm that was perfect for our book photo's.

To all the books, speakers, preachers, works of art, churches, camps, family and friends who filled our minds and spirits with the words that created this book. All of life inspires and transforms our thoughts and opinions. We have two lives worth of inspiration that have found a small place on these pages.

To all of you who supported this project through your contribution on our indiegogo campaign, thank you. This would not have happened without you. Crowdsourcing is a game changer and you have helped change the game. Todd Reynolds both shot and edited the video for this campaign, Laura Mangan stepped in at the last minute of voice overs, and Ryan Workman (https://www.facebook. com/keepyourcourage) let us use his music to underscore the video. This video took our campaign to another level, thank you. Everyone who contributed knows who you are and can find who else supported this project in the wordsearch on the next page.

```
N B D G Y Y N D O F S V G I X T M V K A
A I L I C E C A S S I E E S K L L I B P
L D G O R H S I D C I R T L B A R B K A
E L E A N O R D K G P A A O U K Y Y I E
X C K L U K E I N Y C J N R D L L C O U
N Y L T I A K A S I O D A A K E I T H Z
I Z M B E N C Y E S L E H C A R M A T S
T D C O E Y E C H N Y T T X T O E A G O
S P A I R L D U E N I N A J I B Z K B E
U A N D R E A R S B R E N T E M T U X S
J R A I J C J C A M E L O D Y C O P N G
S A H E L O P T H L F R V D V J S P M O
U S O H V J T A C H P E T S Z Z C M F R
U B Y M H E O H U V O H T U R O N N S A
I M O A R N T R N L F A I C N O H Q C S
G M T B M N V S H O Y J M L R Q C C J S
C H H I V Y M Q Q F A I B P U H I M M I
I I U O I R Y O B R T B E P J A T Z L L
R A C L M G R T L V T L B M W I Y E W E
N Y K J I T X G A T D I S A N M P M U M
```

Dani would like to specifically thank her family who knows about the worst but brings out the best. There aren't enough words to articulate the depth of love for each of you. Thank you for believing in me, sticking with me, forgiving me, loving me, and gracing me with second chances. You embody God's spirit here on earth. To my friends, you fill my heart and complete my soul in a way that I never knew was possible. I couldn't make it through my days without your prayers, your words of wisdom, your laughs and insights. I am blessed to have friends who see me in my glory and my mess and choose to walk through life with me. To my husband Paul, my biggest supporter, you see more in me than I ever believed possible. Thank you for years of grace and love and comfort. You make my story great. To Noah, Caleb, and Eleanor, never have I known the depth of love and fear as I do being your mother. You are my greatest treasures here on earth. I love you and hope to make you proud.

Inga Decker, Sarah Biddix and Ryan Bonfiglio , Heidi Haines, Sara Lightbody, Katrina Hannemann, Kim Waller, Heather Carufel, Lindsey Schmidt, and Chad Amour thank you for stepping in and loving on the kids so that I could make this project happen. You all sacrificed your time and life to help me. Thank you.

Henry Graf, for some reason you choose to stick around in this crazy partnership, and for that I am deeply grateful. Thank you for your commitment to healthy communication and friendships. It is an honor friend.

Thank you Lord for your persistence for my heart. Thank you for life, love and forgiveness. Thank you for giving us the ability to continue your creation with what we create. Thank you for stories that teach us, guide us, encourage us, and inspire us. With you, living this life is a great story.

Henry would like to specifically thank.

1 Corinthians 13:7 says "Love bears all things, believes all things, hopes all things, endures all things" and Mom and Dad, you lived love. It is so much bigger than just Marshall, Amanda, Matthew and me, but the truth remains, "We are one family."

To the three ladies I'm proud share the name Graf with: Tricia, Kaitlyn, and Adeline. You have supported me, encouraged me and sacrificed much, so this project could happen. I can't wait for Sabbath muffins, because they mean I get to share the day with you.

My Almae Matres: Concordia Lutheran High School, Fort Wayne; Indiana University - Purdue University, Fort Wayne and Concordia Theological Seminary, Fort Wayne; as the name suggests you have nourished me well. May this work overflow what you have filled me with.

Ben Sternke for coaching me and introducing me to the 3dm team and Eric Pfeiffer talking me through the "valley of the shadow" over some amazing sushi.

Dani Tietjien, the art of collaboration while difficult is worth it. It is truly an honor to share both the stage and now on the page with you.

Finally, to the Promise Family, thank you for letting me be your Pastor. I am honored and humble by the great gift it is to serve with you. You make stories happen that echo around the world. While I hesitate to name names when I talk publicly of this group, the list is just to long and I will forget to name someone important; yet, Christa Koenemann. Ever since you loaded me into the back of your car and drove me to the ER with a broken neck, you've been saving my life in many and various ways - thank you.

A Story before...

Standing among the white oaks at the 9/11 Memorial in New York City stands a single Callery pear tree, dubbed the 'Survivor Tree'. Reduced to an eight-foot-tall stump, her branches were blackened and her roots were snapped in the 9/11 attacks. Uncovered among the rubble at Ground Zero, somebody saw more than just a burned and broken pear tree – they saw a story.

Inherent in its very existence is a story.

Inherent in our very existence is a story.

We all have countless stories, but sometimes a story becomes more. Some stories transcend geography and echo through eternity; they are so much more that they take on another name.

Sadly, other stories go untold out of fear, shame, or lack of an audience. Worse yet, some stories are not even recognized as stories. But this Callery pear was noticed and recognized and her story is told.

The tree was transplanted to Van Cortlandt Park in the Bronx where the Department of Parks and Recreation nurtured it back to health. Over time, this eight-foot stump grew to stand thirty feet tall with new branches which flowered each spring.

The Survivor Tree had already earned her name when a major storm in March of 2010 uprooted her, but she still had a story to tell. Over the next few months, this Callery pear was moved back to her old neighborhood. The memorial pools stand where the north and south towers fell, their endless depth a fitting tribute to the loss and sorrow. The survivor tree, however, tells another story.

A story of reliance.

A story of hope.

A story of life.

This is not just a story. It is *more than a story*. The story of the

Survivor Tree transcends geography and echoes through eternity. The hope of this book is that the story in you will do the same as you uncover it among the clutter of life.

Stories have power. They hold the ability to influence people and change lives. The stories we live make up the very fabric of our existence. Too often, we miss out on the simple truths found in ordinary stories while we search for the larger, more exciting story. We wrote this book because we believe in the importance of training ourselves to see the depth and truth hidden in the common, everyday stories. We also believe that the full measure of understanding this depth cannot happen without people in our lives. Our stories and their impact hold power within a community where honesty and vulnerability are valued, honored, and desired.

As stories happen, they are brought into existence. Then as it's told, and ultimately as it continues beyond the storyteller into the hearts and minds of those who have received it, it changes and becomes more. This is our hope for the stories that live on these pages and in your hearts. Here, we share stories about our lives and take time to discuss them in a conversational style of writing. We see the ordinary and share in the ordinary, but in that process we unearth **more than just a story**. Most of the stories included in this book aren't big, dynamic, or larger-than-life because most of our lives aren't lived that way. Yet in the conversation that followed each story, we discovered truth, found knowledge, and learned things not only about ourselves and each other, but also about God.

As you read, you will hear two very two distinct voices. This is intentional. As authors we think differently from each other; we approach and understand not only scripture but life in different ways and we articulate and communicate those ideas uniquely. We embrace, welcome and love these differences. While it can be challenging to sit down and invest in someone who thinks differently than you, the reward is worth it. The goal is not to synchronize our voices into one note, but to embrace the differences and in doing so let a harmony emerge.

Our hope is that by sharing these stories with you, the conversation will continue. Stories are meant to be told, and what we learn from them is meant to be shared.

CHAPTER 1:

The Wounded Waitress

~by Dani

Let me tell you about my friend Bill. When we first met, I was 16 years old and one of 800 students who went to Mackinac Island for a youth conference. For five days we would hear motivational speakers, listen to music, take hikes, play card games, attend workshops, and do service projects. On our second night, the band had just finished their set. We had been dancing in the aisles and singing along when the stage lights went dark. The keynote speaker Rev. Bill Yonker was about to take the stage.

We sat there in awestruck wonder as Bill wove stories of deep heartache and courageous victory on the backdrop of the gospel. He spoke of God's unyielding love in a way that made sense to me as it never had before that night. With the ease in which he spoke, I began to understand the depth of God's passion for me. Growing up in the church, I knew grace was the key ingredient to faith, but that night, in that auditorium, it wasn't that God loved all people, it was that God loved me!

He saw me.

He forgave me.

He wanted me.

Christ's gift of the cross was for me.

That night my faith got real and God's love got personal. I was so moved and humbled in my faith by what Bill shared that I begged my mom to go with me and wait in line to see him offstage. At 16, I felt like I was meeting a rock star.

That is who he was to me then.

When I grew up, I wanted to be just like Bill—dynamic, charismatic, and dripping love on everyone who came close. I longed for a relationship with God that, like his, produced such wisdom and thoughtfulness.

Bill is the type of guy who is completely approachable. With his big wide grin, he can fix his eyes on you and make you feel like the only person in the room. His charisma and charm draw you in, creating space for you to be comfortable so that you can have a conversation with him. It was my turn in line and I was nervous as I approached him. Without hesitation, he smiled a 100-watt smile and his friendly eyes sparkled. He stuck out his hand to shake mine, put his other hand on my shoulder, and brought me into his inner circle. He gave me his undivided attention as we spoke and I shared my story with him. He treated me as if I were an old friend. We chatted a few more minutes, and then I went on my way.

Before the conference ended, I saw Bill a few more times, and each time he stopped to call me by name and chat for a few moments. I was blown away that the most sought after man at the conference remembered my name and shared his time with me. This probably wouldn't stand out to Bill because that's just who he is, but for me it is something I will never forget.

Over the next decade, I had dozens of other opportunities to see Bill speak and to share a meal with him. Time grew our small acquaintance into a cherished friendship. The beautiful thing about Bill is that beyond his wisdom, which is deep and rich, he is full of love and attention. He genuinely cares about people and their hurt and pain. He longs to be used by God to bring love here on earth. It is what drew me to him, and why I am so honored to call him my friend.

One spring weekend, Bill and I had the pleasure of working together at a youth conference in Cocoa Beach Florida, much like the one where I met him for the first time. Being on the coast, my mother joined us and we decided to extend our stay until Monday to enjoy a little rest and relaxation.

For dinner on Sunday night, we found a delightful little seafood place with a patio outside facing the ocean. Music played, twinkle lights gave the night a soft glow, and the weather was that ideal mix of warmth on your skin with the brush of a breeze. It was perfect as

we sat outside listening to the waves crash against the shore.

I gazed around and took in the scenery. I was lounging in my chair when I noticed a party of six directly behind us getting up to leave. They collected their coats and purses and started toward the dock and their cars. Once they were away from the table, I watched the waitress come over to clear away dishes and collect the check with its payment. As she was gathering up the money, I watched her double-count it. She looked confused and hurt. Running to catch up with one of the men in the party, she touched him on the arm to get his attention. As he turned, I could tell that she was questioning him about the check, but I couldn't hear what she was saying. It was easy though, at that point, to understand the man as he made sure to yell loud enough for the entire patio to hear.

"You expect a tip? Are you kidding me? You were terrible. The service was slow. You mixed up our drink orders, which we then had to wait for, and our order was wrong. You were a terrible server. You don't deserve a tip!"

My heart hurt so much in that moment. I had been a waitress for a long time and could immediately feel the public humiliation with which this man abused her. In front of everyone, he laid bare her mistakes and poked fun at her. He destroyed her reputation, inviting other customers to pass judgment and cast a vote on whether or not she was worthy. It was wrong and hurtful.

I watched the weight of this man's words rest on her shoulders as she withdrew into herself and sank down into a smaller version of who she was moments before. Her head down, shoulders slumped, she went back to the waitress station.

We all sat a little stunned, no one quite knowing what to do after that. After a few moments, the small talk conversations picked up again, and everyone went about their business as if nothing had happened. Then the people at the table next to us picked up their jackets and headed out to leave. The same waitress came over and started the same routine all over again. She gathered dishes, picked up the check, and for the second time that evening, I could tell by her small reaction, she was stiffed out of a tip. We all heard the heavy sigh. We all saw her shoulders shrink.

And my heart sank, yet again.

She was standing with her back to us, just a couple feet away, and I could feel the sadness and tension radiating off of her. Too broken to chase them and inquire, she slowly put the money away. Then she turned to us with her eyes cast to the ground, apologized for the wait, and asked what she could get us to drink.

Bill, always full of compassion and kindness, reached out and put his hand on her shoulder. He wanted to reassure her that it would be OK and she wasn't alone. He gently asked what her name was, making her a person and not just a servant moving about the patio. Giving her a name, in a small way validated her existence.[1]

She replied quietly, "Theresa."

"Theresa," he said, "We are old friends who never get to see each other; we are just enjoying the company, so please take whatever time you need. When you are ready, we will take a couple of waters."

Off she went, with the three of us never really even seeing her face as she kept it closed off and cast down.

We went about our ordering, our storytelling, our laughs, and our memories throughout the evening.

When our dinner arrived, Theresa had only brought two of the three meals with her. Usually when this situation presents itself, I am stuck with a dilemma. Do we pray while only some people have their food, or do we wait as some watch their delicious meals turning cold? The irony in this is that the server will always be faster than the prayer of thanksgiving. This leaves them waiting awkwardly on the outside of the circle of prayer, holding heavy plates of hot food and feeling out of sorts. They can't put the

food on the table and risk breaking up the circle; so they wait uncomfortably for the prayer to finish.

The other option of waiting for everyone to have their food just causes tension within the group. Those with hot food want to eat, and those without covet those who do. The whole table sits there in uncomfortable silence, waiting and waiting for the rest of the food to arrive. This becomes awkward on all accounts.

When Theresa went away to gather the last dinner, we went for it. We reached out and held hands in prayer.

We prayed for our meal.

We prayed in thanksgiving for the weekend that had just happened.

We thanked God for the stories of healing that occurred in the students' hearts.

Lastly, we prayed for Theresa. We knew she was hurting, and we wanted her to experience God's peace. After the Amen was said, I realized that Theresa was standing there and had heard our prayer. I hoped that she was encouraged rather than offended. From the look on her face, I really couldn't tell.

Our evening continued in great spirits as we laughed and re-connected. Even still, my eyes would wander to the wounded waitress and my heart broke for her.

When our evening was drawing to a close, we got our check and somehow without talking about it, we all had come to the same conclusion. We each wanted to put in a slightly bigger tip than expected. We knew Theresa had been cheated out of money earlier that evening, and while we couldn't cover her entire loss, we could help out if even just a little.

I then sat there, wondering. I knew we could, and probably should just leave the check on the table, but something in me told me to go and give her the money. I wanted to say, "Thank you," one last time and off a genuine smile as a small bit of encouragement. It didn't feel like much, but it felt like the right thing.

I took the check and headed to the waitress station where Theresa was. I stood behind her, and gently said, "Excuse me, Theresa; it was a really wonderful evening. Thank you so much for all you did for us. We had a really great time. This is for you." I then held out our check with its payment. "We wish it could be more."

Theresa turned around and for the first time that evening, she looked at me. I finally saw the eyes of this sad and hurt woman, eyes that overflowed with tears. Looking at her in that moment made me want to join her pain, crying for all the ways she had been mistreated that evening.

Then I realized I was still standing there with my hand out, this woman looking up at me, tears pouring down her face, and I didn't know what to do. She finally grabbed my hands and said, "I have screwed up so badly. I have done so many awful things, and I have fallen away from God. I feel so far from him, and I don't know where he is now."

She didn't say any more.

She just stood there.

Looking at me.

Weeping.

Gripping my hands.

Her very soul exposed and vulnerable and asking me the toughest question there is in life: How can God still love me?

I wish I could say I responded in confidence, ready for this moment. However, what went on inside my head was,

WHAT?!?! Is this really happening to me? You should meet my friend Bill. He's the guy standing over there. Let me introduce you to the nice, educated pastor full of answers and compassion. He would know what to say. Why isn't he standing here? I don't know what to

do? He would be so much better at this than me. What am I going to say? If only it was Bill and not me.

The fact is, I was the one standing there in front of her. I needed to do something, say something, be something for her. She was looking at me, not Bill.

So I took a deep breath, and said this:

"Theresa, take it from someone who knows from experience, there is nothing, and I mean nothing, that you can do that will stop God from loving you. He sees you. He hears you. You are not lost to him. He still loves you."

I thought, *Okay, not bad.*

But she just kept crying. Looking at me, all hurt and sad, and I thought I had blown it. I thought maybe I had said the wrong thing. I didn't know what else to do because those words sum up how I feel about God, but she just kept crying.

I offered to pray with her and she looked up at me with anticipation and said, "YES!" She threw her arms around me and held on tight.

It took me a little bit by surprise, and I thought, "*Well Dani, embrace this moment.*" So I did—PDA and all. My face was quickly drenched from her tears, but I held on and we prayed together. I don't remember what I said, but at the end, we hugged and parted ways.

So here's the point. The moral of the story, if you will:

You will be called upon to do things you don't feel ready for.

But there's more than a moral...

Henry: So what's a story really about? With any story it's easy to get caught up in our favorite details or something we can relate to. Other times we fixate on something we disagree with, because we are looking for a fight. It is often helpful to step back, take a moment, and ask what's the story really about.

Dani: This story is not about a girl praying with a stranger. It does however tell how so often we miss out on special moments of our lives because we don't think we are gifted enough, talented enough, smart enough, eloquent enough, or courageous enough. We are never right enough to be used by God. We play the comparison game and pass the responsibility on to someone else. We see others' gifts and our own shortcomings. We see where they shine and where we lack. We allow excuses to keep us from participating in life changing moments because we are too afraid or too insecure to step out and do something about a situation we see.

Henry: I love when people say things in an eloquent way. In *Akeelah and the Bee* her teacher recites what has become a favorite quote,

> "Our deepest fear is not that we are inadequate. Our deepest fear is that we are powerful beyond measure. It is our light, not our darkness that most frightens us. We ask ourselves, Who am I to be brilliant, gorgeous, talented, fabulous? Actually, who are you not to be? You are a child of God. Your playing small does not serve the world. There is nothing enlightened about shrinking, so that other people won't feel insecure around you. We are all meant to shine, as children do. We were born to make manifest the glory of God that is within us. It's not just in some of us; it is in everyone. As we let our own light shine, we unconsciously give other people permission to do the same. As we are liberated from our own fear, our presence automatically liberates others.[2]"

Dani: So often we think about ourselves, our calling, and what we bring to the table. However, the reality is that it is about the need, and the need is the call. If you see a need in front of you, then God is calling you to do something about it. The brokenness we see presents itself in emotional, mental, spiritual, and physical needs. To respond to these needs, God uses normal, broken people like me and you to reveal His healing power.

Henry: We need to pay attention to the needs that are in front of us. We need to ask what stands out. In this case, Theresa stood out to Dani. It was not the talented and gifted pastor, but Dani— who was still figuring out who she was. It was Dani who didn't have the confidence to talk about her faith with strangers. But she was the one standing in front of Theresa, not Bill. Dani stood there doubting, questioning if she really was the right person to be there. Sure, she doubted she could do it. How often do we all feel that way? How often do we turn and walk away because we don't believe we are the right person to respond to the situation in front of us? The situation that pushes us outside of the comfortable places we have created for ourselves is something we dread. We can always find someone that might be more "qualified," but if we leave the work to them then we simply become observers to our own life instead of full participants. Something miraculous—perhaps even magical—happens when we listen and respond to the need.

Dani: As we pay attention to the needs of others,, we will each be called upon to do things we don't feel ready for. That is after all, the moral of this story. The moral of any story can help us find a piece of truth, encouragement, or challenge. It is why we have added that piece to this book, to help point us to that greater meaning hidden within our stories. By itself the moral is an *addition* to the story; however, it doesn't make it *more than a story*. If you take the time to talk through experiences, you will often find there is even more to the story than you ever anticipated.

Henry: I have had the honor of sharing the stage with Dani as she told this story. I've sat backstage as Pastor Yonker tells the very same story. But it is not the same story. Bill and Dani were at the same restaurant. They had a similar dining experience, but Bill saw something that Dani didn't. As Theresa's tears flooded onto Dani's shoulder and they both closed their eyes to pray, Bill was not caught up in the embrace. He watched the embrace happen and from a distance saw the entire patio bow their heads as Dani prayed. What

Dani perceived as a simple prayer, was so much more.

Dani: When I keep my story to myself, I am sentenced to live with only my perspective. The temptation in this is to believe that my story is small. I can look back on that evening and minimize what happened, believing it was no big deal.

Pretending our stories are small is a way to reinforce the false idea that we are not worthy. We compare the worth of our experiences by measuring them against other people and their stories. In reality however, comparing our experiences as better or worse, more or less, is never fruitful because they are just different. Such comparison is like being original for originality's sake. We stop being original people in our effort to reproduce the life and stories someone else has. As C. S. Lewis beautifully says,

> "No man who values originality will ever be original. But try to tell the truth as you see it, try to do any bit of work as well as it can be done for the work's sake, and what men call originality will come unsought.[3]"

If we only tell the story we find "better" and "more," judging them alone as worthy, some of the best stories could go untold. The beauty in believing your story is worth something allows you to share it. This is the essential difference between the story told in theater and the story told at the table.

I love the idea of the table.

Family and friends gather around it and share sustenance and story. The table combines food, drink, and creates the space for people to connect with each other and allows the sharing of their stories. In my family we share our day's stories over the dinner table. We don't compare who has the better story, or judge who had the most interesting day. We simply desire to know more about each other and to know each other well.

At the table we see that "story" and "life" can be interchanged. The

phrases, "This is the story of my life," or "Let me share my story with you" illustrate this reality. When strung together, the stories we experience make up our life. The reason Henry and I talk about sharing stories and finding worth in our stories is because of this connection between story and life. My story is worth hearing. My life is worth experiencing. When humanity shows up to the table to share life together, we learn from one another and find greater meaning to our stories.

I bring my version of what happened on that patio with Theresa to the table, while Bill brings his perspective to the table. Then, almost magically, we discover a whole new story.

Henry: When people are having a heartfelt interesting conversation at the public table, it gets our attention. We've been taught that it is rude to eavesdrop, so we try our very best to pretend we aren't listening in; but, let's face it, we all do. That night with Theresa, that's what was happening. Everybody who was in the restaurant was eavesdropping as the waitress got bawled out.

Everyone was paying attention as the same waitress poured her tears and her soul out to Dani.

Then when the same crowd heard the whisper of Dani offering to pray with Theresa, they stopped pretending they weren't listening and bowed their heads joining silently in the prayer. We are always surrounded by such a great crowd of witnesses, even when we don't see them ourselves.[4]

Dani had her focus on Theresa, where it should have been, while Bill could watch the rest of the crowd. Dani had her eyes closed as she prayed, but Bill watched and kept his open. We all see different things—that's why we need each other.

Dani: We need other people to help expand and explain the story, to help fill in our blind spots. That evening, one blind spot was the fact that I didn't know the crowd out on that patio stopped to pray with me. I had no idea anyone was paying attention to us.

When you get a new perspective on the story, it gives it a deeper and richer understanding. You see it differently and the story itself changes. I had an even bigger blind spot though, I didn't realize I had a story until Bill pointed it out. On the drive home, he looked at me and said, "That's your story." In the midst of the struggle I didn't see it myself, but I had a story.

Henry: Everybody has a story, from the preschooler on the playground to the soldier returning from the trenches. Many stories are told at a party, or after a day at work, and then quickly forgotten. Some stories are never seen and go untold, while other stories transcend geography and ideology and seem to echo through eternity.

Some are so much more than stories that we call them by other names. No one calls what Aesop, Grimm, or Jesus told stories. We call them fables, fairy tales, and parables.

Dani: Something incredible happens when we talk about our stories. Not just telling the story but really talking through it, allows it to become *more than a story*. Around the table we discover the story in a whole new way. Over time, we discuss words and create a common language that brings understanding to everyone involved. Henry and I had hours of conversation around the words we were using in this book because in a lot of ways, we don't speak the same language.

Henry: When Dani says language, she's not talking about English, Spanish, French, or German. It goes far beyond that. As an American visiting England for the first time, I heard the phrase "We are separated by a common language." This starts to get at the point, but it runs even deeper than boot or trunk, lift or elevator. It breaks into the word's meaning and intention.

I remember my childhood pastor explaining that a parable is "an earthly story with a heavenly meaning." I like that definition because it points to something more. Yet, the "more" can be missed

because the story is lost in the words.

I wonder what the Vegas odds are on you reading "heavenly meaning," and thinking the same thing I intended. I know Dani didn't. We had to talk about it, because "heavenly" is a fairly loaded word. One reader thinks "nice," another thinks "afterlife," while a third thinks "imaginary." This isn't a bad or a good thing. It is simply a real thing. It means that as we live and grow in community, we need to do the hard work of unpacking our language, so that we can understand one another. As a community expands, new conversations need to happen. We need to articulate things we once took for granted because the people who knew us already knew what we intended.

Those who didn't, probably don't.

When I say "heavenly" let's admit that at the very least, I bring all kinds of baggage to the table. I'm working with a set of assumptions that you don't know unless I tell you. Rather than avoid such words, I aim for understanding them. I'll admit, some words have more assumptions and baggage than others, and "heavenly" has a bunch. That's why we will define "heavenly" in a couple of chapters, and a lot of our other key words throughout this book.

When I remember my pastor explaining that a parable is "an earthly story with a heavenly meaning," I liked it because it pointed to something more.

Dani: No one calls it an "earthly story" until something beyond the story is uncovered and unpacked. We've learned that this unpacking happens only through conversations in communities, and it happens best at the table. In each of us is a longing for something more than an earthly story—a better way and heavenly meaning. These types of intentional conversations don't happen overnight, they take time.

Henry: I'll admit that it might seem cheesy, but if you listen to the word "parable," you've already heard what it takes to move from a story to more than a story. When I hear "parable," I hear that it starts with "pair." That is the first step in moving from a story to more than a story; another person.[5] A pair, sitting at the table, telling you their story and talking about yours.

This pair may seem like a small step, but it's necessary.

Solomon was the wisest man ever, and he wrote these words in Ecclesiastes 4:

> Two are better than one,
>> because they have a good return for their labor:
>
> If either of them falls down,
>> one can help the other up.
>
> But pity anyone who falls
>> and has no one to help them up.

Theresa had fallen and Dani was there to help her up. Theresa's story started to become more than a story because of this pair. Pastor Yonker was there to be a pair with Dani. He could point out that she had a story and as they talked about this, her story became richer.

CHAPTER 2:

Frank the Lion Killer

~by Henry

Kaine Prince somehow knew I would struggle to understand his birth name through his thick Ugandan accent. So even his introduction, "Hello, please call me Frank," was gilded with humility and accommodation, the likes of which I'd never experienced before.

I had only vague ideas of what I was in for when I boarded the plane on the morning of my thirty-second birthday. I spent the next twenty-six hours in flight so I could experience South Africa first hand, and sit at the table with students from across the continent at the Theological Seminary in Tshwane. Going in, I knew the six hour time difference between my home and myself, along with my children's bedtimes, and technological issues would make communication with my family very difficult in the weeks to come. But, I am a story collector and this experience was certain to cultivate amazing ones. That along with an unquenchable taste for adventure made this trip irresistible.

We sat in the common area of the dormitory as the heat of the day lifted and I waited, listening expectantly. His elusive accent and broken English served as the backdrop, setting the stage with palpable anticipation. Frank began, "My Pastor told me that I should become a pastor, so I told him that I'd pray about it. I kind of did, but not really."

That is how Frank began his story.

Really?!

Where was the excitement and mystery this continent had promised? Had I really traveled halfway around the world for this?

This story was far too plain, far too common. I had come to collect new stories of intrigue and adventure and heard only the drab recording of so many others with whom I was studying back home.

"My Pastor told me I should become a pastor..." *Yeah, Pastor Hartke told me the same thing during confirmation in 8th grade,* I thought to myself.

I was tired.

I was bored.

I had already heard this story.

Really, I had already told this story.

My mind wandered to the T-shirts I had seen for sale in the airport. I recalled one that said, "My parents went to Africa and all I got was this lousy T-Shirt." Until that moment, I had never understood them. Maybe that was the point both of the shirt and this trip. Then and there I wondered if I had set myself up for failure, expecting too much. Although this continent had promised to be so much, it seemed to be so much of the same. I could have stayed in Indiana and heard the same story.

Maybe it was the jetlag.

Maybe it was the fact that I hadn't slept for over 36 hours, but I was feeling more than a little disappointed. Still, Frank had the coolest exotic accent that I had ever heard, so I attempted to stay tuned in for a few more minutes.

Beside, Tshwane is a little neighborhood in Johannesburg, the murder capital of the world. Since we had been strongly admonished not to leave the gated campus unaccompanied and never after dark, I didn't really have anything else to do. Everyone I knew on the entire continent was sitting right there in the commons with me. So I willed my eyes open and tried to keep listening.

Frank continued, "Then one morning I was walking around, collecting firewood by the side of a creek that had all but dried up. I heard a rustling that I had not heard since my youth. I hardly recognized what it was at first. Then the quiet growl instantly let me know what I was hearing."

As Frank spoke, I started to fade again.

Church people have experiences of the Holy that are often difficult to describe tactilely. Once we move beyond the sensual—what we can see, taste, smell, hear, and feel—we struggle to find aptly descriptive words for these experiences. Yet, the Holy works both within and transcends our five senses. After all, we rightly describe God as Spirit. I'd heard it before, so my thoughts jumped to *the faith of Frank's youth being rekindled, as ever so quietly the Holy Spirit growled within him.*

These long days of travel had caught up with me.

As the heat of the day had cooled from crazy to comfortable, I quickly faded from relaxed to sleepy. I remembered the predawn hours of a cross-country drive and fighting with all I had to keep my eyes open. The feelings were all the same. Then, like the rumble strip on the side of the highway jarring me from my impending slumber, Frank spoke two words and I was wide awake.

"A lion."

The growl he heard wasn't otherworldly at all. With his ears he had heard the growl of a real live lion. In the days to come we would go on safari and see lions, black rhino, zebras, and all kinds of other beasts that I'd only seen behind the bars of a zoo before. Even gazing upon them in the wild, our guide would constantly be on guard and armed with an elephant gun. This was the kind of tale I expected to hear in Africa. Yet, even as I was enlivened by the mere mention of a lion, he calmly continued.

"I saw a tree nearby.

I knew I could climb it quickly.

I ran and the lion ran after me."

Without a variation in tempo or tone he explained that the village had grown larger and gotten louder. When it did, it scared the gazelles far away. Since lions eat gazelles, they followed them away from the village. It had been a very dry summer and the lions were getting restless. Although the creek was all but dried up, they knew the gazelles needed water and this was the most likely source.

"The lions were very hungry," he explained. "When I was a child, they chased us up trees often. It was almost a game to us; but, it has been many years since then. I am very thankful I remembered what to do. Years ago, there was no drought so the lions would go away quickly if we climbed the high tree. But that day, the tree had provided shade from the heat. The lion had not eaten for a long time so he laid at the bottom of the tree waiting for me.

It got very hot in the noonday sun; yet, I did not dare to move.

As the sun went down, the lion paced at the bottom of the tree. He knew I must sleep.

If I sleep, I will fall.

If I fall he will eat me.

So I stayed awake all night and I prayed to my God. I prayed all through the night and as the dawn broke I saw the sun again. That is when I gave up. I prayed 'Dear Jesus, I will die and be with you. I will fall into the mouth of the lion. If you keep me alive I will go away and become a pastor.'

It was with that prayer that the lion heard something.

He turned his head and he ran away."

All the sleep had been vanquished from the room and we sat in silence waiting for whatever words Frank would speak next. One man dared to whisper, "Frank, the lion killer," in the midst of this silence. Then for the first time all evening Frank broke his signature tone of collected calm.

"I was no longer very tired," Frank exclaimed jumping up from the couch as if to illustrate. "I jumped from the tree and ran home to tell my Pastor and my family that I would go to school to be a pastor. I told them that God had rescued me from the lion."

Somehow, after that night the whispered name "Frank the Lion Killer" stuck. No, he never killed the lion; but, we wanted to honor him and the uniqueness of his story. I could embellish, and in my mind often have, that Frank was the lion's last chance at sustenance. That there was no sound far off, but that the lion—due to malnutrition—was hallucinating and hearing things and simply ran off and died. It probably never happened that way; but, it is fun to imagine.

Oddly enough, when Frank went home between semesters, he told his friends what the American's had called him and the nickname stuck even there. My friend is now Pastor Kaine Prince and he faithfully serves the people of Kampala, Uganda; but to me he will always be "Frank, the Lion Killer."

So here's the point. The moral of the story, if you will:

> When a story is observed from afar,
> the differences are often seen as "more."

But there's more than a moral...

Dani: Stories from around the world are exciting and enticing. No one goes around my neighborhood facing off with lions. Modern technology has now brought the far reaches of the world and stories like this one to our door steps. We can be knowledgeable about countries we've never been to without even getting up off the couch. This puts an interesting spin on the words of Jesus,

"You will be my witnesses in Jerusalem, and in all Judea and Samaria, and to the ends of the earth."[1]

The ends of the earth are closer than they ever have been. It is easier to get there and raise our understanding of cultures and people we have never met. We are drawn to exotic places that stretch our imagination, and to the people who are vastly different from us. There is something distinctly romantic about traveling to the ends of the earth, especially when it's to help the orphans and the widows, the slaves and the abused. It seems enticing to get up, sell everything, and move across the globe to help those who have been ravaged by a natural disaster or civil war. That we could be the voice of the voiceless children in Africa or fight for the unseen women in India. Their stories are filled with great despair and heartache and unimaginable pain and injustice. We are drawn to these stories because they are larger than life.

It would be a tragedy however to only see those great big stories that come from distant places while ignoring the neighbor down the street, or the kids in the local school that are homeless and hiding. It doesn't sound as exciting to make a meal for a single mom as it does to serve on a mission trip for a week in a third world country.

However, that dinner is a major story to the mom who is at the end of her rope wondering how to make ends meet. As she wonders how to keep working two jobs and still somehow be there for her kids, that meal feels like a thousand bucks. That meal validates her pain and her existence.

That meal itself is more than a story.

She feels seen and loved.

That bit of encouragement is enough to help her move forward and not give up. It is enough of a reprieve after working long hours to have more patience and love for her kids. Serving and loving and really engaging the people who look and live and sound like us, is where the real story starts. The people who live close to us still need our help—and we need theirs. We need each other to see the pain and the needs that we can't meet on our own. Simply put, we need pairs.

If we are caught up in the romantic idea of all the faraway places, then we miss what is happening right in our own neighborhood.

Henry: I've never raised money more quickly and easily than when

I traveled to Africa. What I've noticed is it is a lot easier to get people interested in those far off and fantastical ends of the earth places than it is to get them interested in Jerusalem. Even though to us Jerusalem seems very "ends of the earth," it is essential to remember who Jesus was talking to. Only then can we understand what He was truly saying.

When Jesus' disciples heard him say, "Jerusalem" they heard, "right where you are, where the people are a lot like you." In Jerusalem the people ate the same foods, played the same sports, and listened to the same music[2] as the disciples did. Judea was a little bit further away, but the people were still ideologically and culturally similar. The difference between Jerusalem and Judea was simply geography. For them Jerusalem was where they could easily walk, but they would prefer to ride a camel and needed to bring some water when going to Judea. While we may not ride camels today, the point is the same. Your school, office, or neighborhood is your Jerusalem. These are the places where you can walk or easily drive to; but to get to Judea you need to drive much further and you might even need to fly.

With the relative ease of commuting and advances in technology, it is easy to miss and minimize the huge role geography plays in the stories we tell. What we don't realize at first glance is that when we attempt to share Judea stories the physical distance between us and them matters. In Jerusalem such distance just isn't the case. It is essential to neither underestimate nor minimize the implications and insulation of geography. The insulation is likely the more important of the two.

This is the simplest illustration of how distance insulates us: If there is a story that I don't want to hear being told in Judea, I can very easily avoid hearing it. Such insulation is not as easy in Jerusalem. If I don't like you or your story, but you are in my Jerusalem, I'll probably still bump into you. While I'd have to actively avoid those in my Jerusalem, I have to actively interact with my Judea.

Geography is the difference between Jerusalem and Judea.

If you look on a map, you'd notice that both Judea and Samaria are about the same distance from Jerusalem. Yet, Jesus lists them both separately. The reason for this is because Samaria is separated from Jerusalem both geographically, but also culturally. In Judea the people are like you, just further away. In Samaria they eat different foods, play different sports, and listen to different music, while still living farther away. These people are intriguing—especially when kept at a distance—but they seem so weird.

Then Jesus moves to "the ends of the earth," a bit more ambiguous term, where the other is even farther away and culturally more different. Everything about these people and the place where they live is different. They look different, their language is different, their food is interesting, and their clothes are intriguing. There is something fantastical about far off places, simply because it is so far from our own reality. As I've reflected, I realize that is why I was initially so disappointed with the start of Frank's story. I was expecting an ends of the earth story, but it was too much like mine.

Dani: "Too much like mine." These words hit a weak and tender spot in my self-awareness. I also believe it sits at the crux of why we so often choose the "ends of the earth" over Jerusalem. It starts to speak to the judgment and selfishness that lives in each of us. It can be difficult to invest in people that live in your Jerusalem. In this, I don't merely mean existing with other people, and sharing activities with them. It means, "loving you is going to be hard." It will require that I give of my time and energy to be there for you in a way that you need me. It is a courageous act of investing your truest self in showing up, being present, and giving everything you have to people who live in your Jerusalem.

This is difficult because you aren't just visiting your Jerusalem, you live in it. The needs of the people around you don't go away, which

inherently means you are committed to these relationships in a way that you can't be to those who live at the ends of the earth. Living in Jerusalem, relationships require more from us. In turn, we are drawn to the cultures we don't understand because there is mystery around them. They require less from us, although the dramatic stories we hear from these faraway places speak to our need for our shared humanity, those things we all have in common.

Henry: Even the language we use to talk about engaging the ends of the earth betrays our desire to keep shared humanity at arms length. Keeping the economic poverty confined to an ends of the earth Haiti, insulates me from my own relational poverty. The ends of the earth fear and intrigue of being chased by a lion is compartmentalized to Africa and inasmuch I can compartmentalizes my own fear, ultimately exiling them to a far off place. Then, when we do interact with the ends of the earth, we say things like, "We are going to pour out ourselves to these people."

I know there is Biblical language of pouring oneself out as a drink offering[3]; but Jesus doesn't speak of pouring out in this text. The way we talk about something does affect how we experience it. Whether it is at the front of our minds or not, when we say "pour out" we know deep in our belly that when the pouring out is done, whatever is poured out from will be empty. If I pour my coffee cup out, I don't expect to have anything left when I'm done. The concept of me being poured out, especially to something as different and far away as the ends of the earth, is both scary and unsustainable. Rather than "pouring out into" the ends of the earth, a model of emptiness, a more sustainable concept is overflowing.

I'd call this kind of engaging in Jerusalem "living fully." When we live fully in Jerusalem, our story will naturally overflow into the same kind of engagement with Judea. As the filling and overflowing continues, Samaria is filled then to the ends of the earth. Such overflowing is a very different picture than pouring out. It leaves us with a different sense all together. Unfortunately, we can't overflow until we have been filled up by engaging fully in our Jerusalem.

Dani: Growing up, my Jerusalem was just outside of Detroit. My Dad was a cop, my mom was my youth director, my older sister was the neighborhood babysitter, and my little brother lived out his role of generally being a pain in the butt. My dad worked midnights in the police department. It was fun and terrifying to have a dad as a police officer. On one hand, I had my own personal body guard to help me out if I ever found myself in a dangerous situation. The reverse of that statement is equally true, as I had my own personal watchdog. He knew what was going on at all times with me and my friends. Working midnights, I couldn't miss curfew or he would know.

On Friday nights when the family would be watching a movie, my dad would pull out all of his tools and weapons and guns and clean them. He would drive me to Junior High pulling up to the school in his squad car and open the back door so I could get out like a criminal, guaranteeing that I would have to give him a kiss goodbye. I think it was his way of making a statement, "Don't touch my daughter, or I'll come after you."

It worked.

Telling stories of robbers, knife fights, car chases, and murders were nothing out of the ordinary around our dinner table. One time, the words, "Did I ever tell you about the decapitated head lady?" came out of my dad's mouth. Instead of being offended, we sat enthralled with the story, hanging on every gory detail and description that he was legally allowed to share. I never thought any of this was strange until I brought a few friends home from college. They sat stunned as he cleaned his weapons and told his stories. This was not normal for them.

With my dad's job, we were able to see firsthand how the story of Jesus and God's love played out in our everyday life. I learned

quite a lot about the law and mercy, grace and punishment, and consequences; all from listening to my dad tell stories. These are high church words, but with my dad and his job, it always meant something more to me. "Witness" is another word that resonates differently with me. When Jesus says, "You will be my witnesses in Jerusalem," it often scares people. Witness has been associated with a large education, confidence in your faith, and a strong knowledge of scripture. I don't believe this is what Jesus meant when he spoke those words.

Jesus' disciples were the men who no Rabbi would take. They were not intellects who spent all their time studying theology and faith. They had already left school to take up the family trade. Most were your standard "every man," except for the one who was in the Militia. They were normal, low educated, hard working men (except for the tax collector, a profession known as lazy swindlers) who Jesus pulled out of their field and said, "Follow me." He calls to them and says, "You will be my witnesses." You have a story to tell.

According to my dad, and what I learned from him, witness really just requires that you share the story of what you saw or experienced. It needs nothing other than your honesty. If we think about witness in that way, Jesus' words are simply asking that we share what we know with the people we live with. We can all do that. He wanted his own disciples to share their story with everyone who would listen.

Henry: As the disciples' witness overflowed from Jerusalem to Judea, then to Samaria, and is continuing even today to the ends of the earth it has become more than a story. Fables, fairy tales, and parables are all more than a story, but why does each transcend?

Both fables and fairy tales come from far off "ends of the earth," or even otherworldly places. There is magic and mystery aligned with each one. They are steeped in imagination and told with a sense of the unknown. Aesop has over 655 fables each with their iconic talking animals. Part of the "more" of his story is simply that animals don't talk—at least not in Jerusalem. Fairy tales push even further into the ends of the earth. They don't merely have ordinary animals doing extraordinary things; the brothers' Grimm invented extraordinary animals. Part of the "more" in a fairytale is the creature itself. They use witches in enchanted castles and flying, fire-breathing dragons. Fables and fairy tales are certainly more than stories, and so is a parable. Yet, a parable has none of these "ends of the earth" or otherworldly elements.

It is why I have grown to love them.

They speak of a world that does exist and one that I understand, while still carrying power to inspire me. As we engage with Jerusalem, parables can emerge.

Dani: From the stage, Henry's and my stories sound like "ends of the earth" stories and some of them from Africa and Haiti really are. Most of the stories in this book however, are Jerusalem stories. Like Jesus, they are stories of real people in everyday events. One of the things I love about the parables that Jesus told is how it reinforces God's love for ordinary people. He knows intimately the mundane experiences that make up our lives; the simple things that happen throughout the day. He uses those moments to create his stories. Jesus spoke of lost coins, sheep, farmers, women who lost their husbands, and children who ran away from home.

It is important though to recognize that these everyday experiences serve as the material for the story. Jesus' parables have been told and retold for over 2,000 years, but that is not what makes them "more." What makes a story *more than a story* is not the story itself nor its retelling, but the discussion that flows from it. It is in talking about the story with each other that we find its meaning and truth; the pieces that impact and change our life.

You need to know that you have a story.

We all do.

There are stories that live within each of us if we dare to share our voice with one another.

Henry: In *The Orthodox Heretic*, after a rather detailed exposition and definition of what parables are, Peter Rollins ends the introduction of his book saying,

> "So, I find myself compelled to end with a prayer of sorts, one in which I express my hope that these tiny tales will become more than mere words on a page to you the reader, perhaps even becoming worthy of the title parable. But, at the end of the day, that is for you to decide."

This begs the question, how do we decide?

Could Frank's story, or Rollins' "tiny tale," become more than a story?

When Frank told his story, it started to. This was simply because it had a man interacting with a lion—to me a fanciful otherworldly beast. The lion drew me in. Perhaps it made his story more of a fairy tale. Had the lion talked, it might have become a fable. But these "end of the world" elements are flimsy and weak in comparison to the power of parable discussed in Jerusalem.

It is not the fact that the stories herein are written in a book that will make them more than a story, but such transcendence happens only when you discuss them.

CHAPTER 3:

I Cleaned My Plate

~by Henry

One night, when I was just a little boy, my mom made my favorite dinner. It wasn't my birthday. No special guests were invited. I hadn't gotten a good grade or finished first in a race; but just to see me smile, mom made all my favorites.

Potato Pancakes,

Homemade Applesauce,

Pot Roast,

and then she messed the whole thing up…with Peas.

I put the homemade applesauce on the potato pancakes and devoured them. I asked for another pancake just to sop up the gravy left on the plate from the pot roast that I inhaled moments before. Mom began to get up from the table and said, "I've made a special dessert too. Just finish your peas while I get it."

With that, mom left the room. I gazed down at my peas and they stared back at me. That is when I had an epiphany.

Do you remember those "shape block boxes" from when you were a kid? It was basically a bunch of blocks of different shapes and sizes then a wooden box with holes cut out. Each hole was cut to fit a block. Hours and hours of fun, right?

This toy is designed for a very young child. It is meant to teach them spatial reasoning; that certain shapes and sizes fit together.

The triangle block fits in a triangle hole.

The square block in the square hole.

The circle block in the circle hole.

However, I quickly learned that if you take the triangle and twist it in just the right way, and apply just a little more force, it will fit in the hole designed for the octagon. I took this as a personal challenge and once I discovered the hammer in dad's workshop, it was "game on."

I could fit almost any block in almost any hole.

Peas, those little spherical balls, are not mouth-shaped. There was another hole however, less than an inch away from my mouth, into which peas fit perfectly. So, as my mother prepared my dessert in the other room, I put the peas in their proper place.

I could fit about three peas in each nostril before I had to apply any pressure. By the time my mom returned, prepared with her bribe but ready for battle, she looked at my plate and smiled. "You cleaned your plate!" she exclaimed.

We both smiled as I devoured my dessert.

Later that evening Mom was getting me ready for bed. She said, "You sound a bit stuffed up."

I quipped back, "I didn't stick anything up my nose."

Nervously she gave me a look. Actually, it was "the look." The one that all moms give their children. The look that screams *I know what happened, but I'm praying it is not as bad as I know it will be.* So, she bit her lip, gave me that look and said, "Well, let's blow it anyway."

I've never known why moms do this, but my mom did and I've found out since then that all moms do...they open the tissue and look into it. Most nights, I wondered what she expected to find. But that night, I knew.

Mom looked at me and calmly asked, "Did you stick peas up your nose?"

Filled with shame, I nodded my head up and down as I whimpered, "Naaaaa-yes." I've never been able to lie to my mom—at least not for very long.

Mom inquired, "How many peas did you stick up your nose?"

With hands on my hips, I proudly proclaimed, "I cleaned my plate!"

So, it was off to the emergency room.

I nervously shivered on the paper-lined, adjustable bed for what seemed like hours, until the doctor finally walked in. He looked at my intake chart and asked if I had really put peas up my nose. I said nothing, but nodded yes. He asked if I knew I wasn't supposed to put things into my nose and my chagrined, silent head-shaking continued.

On any other night, mom would have urged me to speak saying, "We can't hear your brains rattle," but that night she stood in silence. She was the mom, who had the boy, who stuck peas up his nose. As mom looked on and the silence screamed, the doctor continued explaining.

He was going to put a big metal straw up my nose. This was hard for my childhood mind to comprehend, since moments before he had chastised me for putting things in my nose. The straw was hooked up to suction, kind of like a vacuum cleaner and it would suck the peas out of my nose. I nodded in agreement and understanding.

It sucked the peas.

It felt like it was sucking my eyes out of their sockets. Some have argued that it might have sucked the brains out of my head, which would explain a lot.

Let's just leave it at this: his description was spot on. It sucked. But, it did the job.

Mom and I walked out to the car. She opened the hatchback, but before I could climb in she got down on her knee and looked at me straight in the eye. She said, "Henry, you do some stupid stuff."

I didn't interrupt or argue, but pitifully nodded my head, sadly and repeatedly, in agreement. Then she stretched out her arms and reminded me of the most basic truth, "But you're my boy, and I love you."

So here's the point. The moral of the story, if you will:

> Everyone has things they don't like,
> hiding them is not the solution.

But there's more than a moral...

Dani: This story reminds me of a morning when I drove my husband Paul to work. We weaved our way through the busy streets of North Minneapolis. I reached over to hold his hand while we sat, waiting for the light to turn green. Sitting there, I noticed an elderly gentleman slowly making his way through the crosswalk. What was left of his hair had turned grey, and he wore a baggy sweater that wrapped around his frail frame. He leaned heavily on his cane for support as we watched him shuffle his feet to keep himself upright. That was when I noticed the empty, dented soda can. This gentleman was carefully and strategically kicking the can across the street with his cane.

Slowly, carefully he knocked the can to move it in front of him.

Clumsily and awkwardly he would miss and try again.

Moments passed, the light turned green, and still his head was lowered to concentrate on what he was doing. He had committed himself to moving this old soda can from one end of the street to the other. Failure was not an option, and neither was bending down to pick it up.

For a moment I thought, *"Maybe I should get out and help him,"* but I was mesmerized by his attention to this beat up piece of trash.

Long moments later, he arrived to the other side of the street. There was a trash can on that corner, a bus stop bench and a few bushes planted for scenery. It only made sense that this little old man, who after such a long and strenuous walk across the street, was going to dispose of the can in the garbage.

Instead however, Paul and I watched him knock the can under the bush with his cane and keep shuffling down the street.

Paul looked at me and said, "Did you just see what happened"?

It was incredible. All that time, all the struggling and hobbling, the strategic hitting with his cane to move the garbage out of the street, only to hide it under the bush. It made me think of the things I like to hide. I reflected on the large amount of time and energy I invest in the process of hiding and keeping stuff hidden instead of just dealing with it.

Garbage hidden under a bush is still there. It was never cleaned up. It was never taken care of. The gentleman didn't get rid of the garbage. At most, all he did was kick it around a little and then hide it, pretending no one else saw it.

We saw it.

Paul and I knew it was there.

In fact, every person that walked by that bush saw it. The only one who thought that maybe it was hidden, was the man who hid it. But remember, hiding doesn't work.

Henry: The moral of this story is not a new one at all. Growing up I went to a liturgical church where each week we would repeat the words of the Apostle John,

> If we say we have no sin we deceive ourselves and the truth is not in us; but, if we confess our sin God is faithful and just to forgive our sin and cleanse us from all unrighteousness.[2]

I recited those words week after week, but never understood them; at least not until I read the story of Achilles.

Achilles mom, Thetis, was told that if she dipped him in the Styx (the river, not the band), wherever the water touched his body would be protected from all harm. So she grabbed her son by the ankle and dipped him, face first, into the river. The only place where the water didn't touch him was the heel she was holding onto. In Greek, the word *"hamartia"* is used to describe his heel.

It tripped him up.

It was the place where he was vulnerable.

It was his area of weakness.

This word, *hamartia*, gets translated as "sin" throughout the Bible. As a child I thought sin was the thing I did wrong: saying a dirty word on the playground or sneaking a sip of peach schnapps in my buddy Steve's basement. While sin includes these things, it is also so much more.

This bigger word, *hamartia*, is what John wrote in the Bible and I repeated week after week in the liturgy. Even though I had not understood what I was reciting at church, I lived it nonetheless. That's what I was attempting when I stuck those peas up my nose.

If I knew then, what I know now, I would paraphrase 1 John 1:8 like this and repeat it daily:

> If I say I have no weakness, no area of vulnerability, nothing in my life that I'm ashamed of and hurt by, the only one who is really being deceived is me. Everybody else sees it. They may not be able to put their finger on exactly what it is, but they know something doesn't sit right and it drives a wedge between them and me. This hiding also drives out Jesus, who told us He is the way, the truth, and the life.

Dani: It may seem that the issue of hiding the broken pieces of who we are is irrelevant, or over-communicated. Don't we already know that hiding doesn't work? That pretending to be something other than what we are is in itself a sign of weakness? Still, it takes courage to own who we are.

It is hard to be vulnerable.

Hiding is our human response to guilt and shame.

We don't talk about it.

We ignore it.

We distract ourselves so we don't have to deal with it.

It doesn't matter if its peas or garbage, the lies you told, that thing you stole, or that person you hurt, even when it's hidden, it is still there.

Adam and Eve are a perfect example of this. They had lived in open community with their Creator; hiding nothing. As the first people to walk the earth, they hid at the first sign of brokenness because they were afraid to admit their mistake.

Henry: Adam and Eve hid from God[1], but before they hid, we see that they clothed themselves, attempting to hide their nakedness from each other and even themselves. This part of the Bible was first written in Hebrew and in that language, the word "clothed" is the same root word as "deceived." That concept makes total sense when we think about it. As we cover parts of ourselves that we don't want others to see, we are attempting to deceive them.

Dani: Ashamed and guilty, Adam and Eve tried to hide their mistake, the wrong they committed, the brokenness of the relationship between them and God. Henry tried to hide peas, the thing he didn't like, and the man on the street fought to hide the garbage. Somehow we believe that if we hide it, then it makes it like it never happened, like it isn't even there. If you can't see it, or know what my sin is, then it doesn't have a name and it isn't validated. This translates into not just deceiving others, but like Henry said, we ultimately are deceiving ourselves. We continue to try to convince ourselves that we are the person we present to others. We attempt to make that true, instead of living fully as we are, the good, the bad, and the broken mess. Now there are parallel ideas happening. We have clothing that hides us from others, while simultaneously we deceive ourselves about who we really are. So when are we ever truly just being ourselves? And how long can you deceive yourself before you forget who you were created to be?

Henry: That sounds like Hell, doesn't it?

One of my friends found out that his wife had been cheating on

him with another man. He knew their marriage wasn't perfect, but he never expected that. As we continued talking, he explained how he found out about the affair. He thought nothing of the extra car parked in the driveway, they had friends visit often. This added to the shock, when he walked into the house he found them in the midst of the act on the living room sofa. As he told the story, I couldn't read his emotions—in hindsight I realize he was still numb, so I asked how he was doing with all of this. He replied, "Dude, this is Hell."

Another friend enlisted in the military. He really wanted to go to college but couldn't afford it. The recruiter told him he'd never deploy. He would do his for four years and college would be paid for. The week of his graduation from boot camp was the same week as 9/11 and he deployed shortly thereafter. He only talks about what happened on that deployment after he's had one too many, but when he looked me in the eye and said "War is Hell," it was a sober statement.

I've taken many mission trips to countries where the corrupt government keeps their people living in complete poverty without food, clean water, education, or medical care. Each time I go, someone on the trip sees this system and utters the words "They live in Hell."

Dani: We all have experienced some form of Hell. Your immediate reaction to that might be denial, but think about it. If you have ever been affected by the loss of a loved one, abuse, neglect, low self-esteem, or loneliness (the list is endless) then you might have even uttered the words, "This feels like Hell," yourself.

Henry: We all, at one time or another have thought, "It just shouldn't be like that." Rape, violence, genocide, and all the things Dani mentioned above—these are all fruit from the kingdom of Hell. When I talk about Hell, I'm talking about these things and all the ways it shouldn't be. That's what I mean when I say Hell.

When pressed, we all agree there is a way; actually lots of ways, it shouldn't be. We long for something more than Hell, even if we doubt it can exist.

My friend longs for fidelity in his marriage.

The people in poverty long for clean water and full stomachs.

The soldier longs for peace.

Deep in your gut, you know it and deep in your heart you long for it. I know I do. We long for something; well, heavenly. There is the story, and there is *more than a story*, a heavenly meaning. When I say "heavenly," that is what I'm talking about.

The better way.

The way it was meant to be.

Heavenly meaning is moving toward that better way. It is a way that brings love, peace, hope, forgiveness, and grace.

Dani: "Because with every action, comment, and conversation, we have the choice to invite Heaven or Hell to earth."[3] I believe this statement to be true. Isn't this what Jesus taught us to pray for when He said, "Thy kingdom" (that is, the heavenly kingdom) "come, thy will be done on earth as it is in heaven?" We bring destruction or healing in our words. We invite hope or hurt in our actions. There is Heaven and there is Hell and with everything we do we usher in one or the other.

A better way cannot be found though, if we are hiding behind guilt, shame, and embarrassment. There are times when we do not like what we've done, or what has been done to us. We wish we could make it go away. We do not want to expose it, or deal with it, because then others would see our weakness. Our fear then is that we would become less to them, less than whole.

I choose the word "whole" because as a culture I recognize that we understand we are not perfect. Thanks to John Mayer, embracing

our lives as "beautiful messes," is currently in vogue. While this is an important start, our brokenness cuts deeper than a mere 140 characters only to be swept away with the next tweet. I do however believe that we desire to be whole; fully complete and healed. We know in our heads and hearts that we cannot be perfect. If we are truthful, we recognize that it is acceptable for others to be a mess, but cannot accept this for ourselves. We won't admit to striving towards perfection, though we can confess to the desire to be more.

Admitting to this brings out the fear that if all you see are the cracks in my strength, the places that are dark in my heart, and the thoughts that won't flee my mind, then you won't see anything else.

You won't see me.

This then reveals my deepest fear; that you won't want me.

Being wanted and accepted by someone is a deep human need. Though we long for it, we are afraid that our baggage is too much. That we now are too broken to be completely and honestly who we are.

We ask ourselves "What if I risk showing you the darkness and you leave?"

The risk of that kind of honesty feels too great, so we don't take it. We then live hiding and pretending until no one really knows us, fearful that our brokenness makes us less than whole.

Henry: I don't think it's too far of a stretch to connect this kind of whole-ness and holiness. There is a huge gap between the heavenly, holy, wholeness that we long for and the experience we are living. I call this place, the space between heaven and hell "the bull."

I like to use that word for a couple of reasons. First, it's not "dirty," but it gets to the point. A child can understand it. Albert Einstein once said, "If you can't explain it to a six year old, you don't understand it yourself."

There is a legend that Einstein once sat in on a lecture at a prestigious university that happened to be on one of his own highly complex theories. After the professor had lectured for hours—filling the board with complex equations, and thoroughly confusing the class of brilliant PhD students—the professor noticed Einstein, sitting in the back of the room. Upon recognizing him, the professor concluded his lecture and announced to the class that the man who penned this theory was among them.

The professor asked, "Do you sir, have anything to add?"

Albert walked to the front of the room, erased the board and drew a simple picture of a train car and a single directional arrow. In a few moments, by telling a story of a boy playing with a ball on a train, the class understood and sat in awe.

That class needed the simple drawing to understand the complex theory. The drawing worked as a hook on which all the complexity could hang. Growing up in a tidy home, I understood the concept of hooks. There was a place for everything, and everything had its place.

When I graduated from high school and spent my first summer as a camp counselor, I was appalled at how messy a few fourth and fifth grade boys could be. During my first week shirts, shorts, and swimsuits were strewn around the cabin. On Friday, after all the boys had gone home, I found smelly socks and dirty underwear they had left behind. A wet towel had been left on the top bunk and had already started to mildew. I had no idea things could get so gross so quick. Even the smell was horrible. I was still frustrated after I had done my laundry and was putting it away. That's when I realized, the boys had no place to put all their stuff. There was no place for anything, so everything was out of place.

So I drove to the hardware store and bought about 25 hooks and a clothes line. I tied the clothesline outside between two trees. This solved the cluttered swimsuit and mildewy towel problem; however,

it almost caused a decapitation problem when we were running full speed through the camp the first night (but that's another story altogether). Then I filled the wall with hooks. On the first night of camp; rather than telling the boys we needed to keep our cabin clean, I gave them a tool and said, "Hang your clothes up on these hooks, throw your dirty clothes in a plastic bag, and keep them in your suitcase. We are going to win the clean cabin award this week." It might sound too simple, but it worked.

So often, when I'm not living *more than a story*, it is because I've forgotten the parable hooks. I'm trying to do it by myself, or hide myself from others, rather than hanging my story on the hook of "pair." Other times, I close my eyes to the hook of "bull," pretending that everything is perfect even when I know that it's not. I'll never see *more than a story* without hanging my life on these two simple hooks.

Dani: It's important to realize that relationships can have eyes to see past what we present to others and to see us for who we really are. It never ceases to amaze me that what I've tried to hide, my pair already knew. They may not know the details, but at a gut level they knew. Henry's mom may not have seen where the peas went, but she knew something wasn't right.

It would be easy to just pass this off as a normal tale between a mom and son. As a mother, I have countless stories of spills, accidents, and incidents between my kids. Fights, make up's, fort building, errand running, and chore duty are all the things that make up my life. So often it becomes easy to miss the story in the moments of ordinary living. When life gets so busy that we don't have time, or we refuse to take the time to reflect on them.

We take pause over this story. When we take a moment, together we see that there is something beautiful. Aside from all the things we have discovered here, this is a story where a kid does something stupid, like every kid does a thousand times over. Henry's mom,

seeing that her son made a mistake and that he suffered the consequences, took that moment to see him in his mistake, in his sin, and reminded him that he is loved.

She didn't say, "Everything is going to be OK."

She didn't say, "I told you so."

She didn't even say, "Don't ever do that again."

She simply said, "I love you. I saw the stupid thing you did, and I love you."

Finished.

If we didn't take a moment to stop and reflect on this story, then it would just be about a mom loving her son. There's even more to the story than that. The greater meaning in this story is that even when what we are hiding is exposed, or our secret revealed, or mess discovered for everyone to see—love is greater.

Love is always stronger and more powerful than the junk we hide.

CHAPTER 4:

It's Just My Face

~by Dani

I loved growing up on the outskirts of Detroit. There were bike trails, the theater, and the historic Tigers Stadium. As a teenager, part of the lure for Detroit was how easily you could cross the border to go into Canada. My family had a cabin there where we spent every available moment during the summer. It was a quaint little community built at the end of a gravel road. There was one local corner store where you could purchase bait for fishing and snacks for the boat.

The lake was hidden and perfect.

We would chase butterflies in the sunshine, catch frogs down by the water on cloudy days, and skip rocks when we got bored. We would invite friends for the weekend and play volleyball, card games, take boat trips, and spent hours riding the jet skis.

My cousins and I were maniacs the way we challenged each other in game after game of chicken. We would see who would let go first, or who could get their passenger to fall off the back. Last one still dry, or still driving, was the winner. Sometimes just doubling over in laughter caused us to stop. Our competitions became increasingly fierce and reckless. Those moments were more fun than anything else I can remember.

My childhood summer days are filled with beautiful memories like these in Canada. The year I turned 16, my folks, my friend Becky, and I went to the cabin for a day trip. My parents spent their time completing chores around the yard, while Becky and I decided to take the jet ski out.

At the cabin, we have a rule regarding the water. Actually we have several rules, but this is the most important one:

Never go alone.

When you are out on the water, you cannot at any point be out there by yourself. You need a partner; it is the golden rule of safety.

Out on the water, Becky and I were having a blast. At one point, I

dropped her off at the beach to take the jet ski out for a quick spin. The water was crystal clear, the waves had gentle rolls to them, and the wind was mild. It was a perfect day to be out on the water. I used my time on the jet ski to learn new maneuvers and practice my jumps.

Before heading back in to give Becky a turn, I saw a large boat leaving the harbor that created the perfect wave for my last jump. I spun around to give myself enough room to hit full speed as I met their wake. Approaching the boat, I was half squatting to withstand the impact. I crouched low to bring the jet ski up to my chest so I could reach the optimal height in my jump. I was right on the edge when I saw exactly how deep the wake was. I didn't know how to get out, it was too deep and the wave too high for any jumps I felt safe with. Sitting on the wave's edge, I was already committed. There was no turning back.

I was terrified as I was suspended in mid air, until I started my descent back to the lake. My body collided with the jet ski and I felt the impact hit me straight in the stomach, slam my shoulder, and crush my face.

As I came up from the water, my head was pounding.

There was blood all down the front of my chest.

I instantly felt an empty space where my front teeth should have been.

With the small amount of strength I could find, I rolled the jet ski upright, grabbed the strap and pulled myself up. Once I was sitting on the jet ski, I put my head down on the handlebars and watched the blood stream down from my face and cover the seat. Everything on my face hurt, so I wasn't quite sure where the blood was coming from.

With shaky hands, I put the key back in and pointed the jet ski in the direction of the beach where Becky was waiting, praying I could

make it that far. I don't remember much after that. I do know Becky got me back home, and when I woke up I was in the local hospital with a neck brace.

Lying on the clinic's bed, I took inventory of all the different places where my body hurt. My face was throbbing with pain. It felt so severe that I couldn't even hold my head up.

I had a hard time using my left arm for a while. There was a bruise that wrapped from the front of my chest to my back shoulder blade. My eyes had dark circles under them, and my nose, though not broken, was almost twice its normal size. You could see the imprint of the handlebars across my stomach. Even with all this pain, the only permanent damage was to my mouth.

After a week of lying in bed and healing, I got my first retainer with fake teeth. Because of the extensive damage, this was the temporary solution to hold me over till the rest of my mouth healed and I could sustain a more permanent surgery. I'm fine today; but it took five years and multiple experimental procedures before everything was finally fixed.

So here's the point. The moral of the story, if you will:

> Never go alone, in the water or in life.

But there's more than a moral...

Henry: The first time I met Dani, I heard this story, not because Dani spends her days telling that story over and over, but out of necessity. I was living in Dallas at the time and my friend Paul brought his new girlfriend home to meet his inner circle: family and hometown friends. If you've seen the hometown date episode on "The Bachelor," you know what I'm talking about. You don't bring a girlfriend home until you are pretty serious and thinking about taking the relationship to the next level. So, Tricia and I met up with them at Chili's.

We started off with an appetizer, which was a big deal at this point

of all our lives because Tricia and I were broke. The appetizer is what set that meal off as significant. It made a meal fancy, and that day we went big—the Triple Dipper Tower: Boneless Buffalo Wings, Southwestern Eggrolls, and Mozzarella Sticks.

I knew my job on the hometown date episode. We all had a role to play, and mine was protective friend. I had to watch out for my boy. Dani seemed nice and all, but when she took a Mozzarella Stick from the Triple Dipper Tower and used a fork and a knife to eat it, a red flag went off. "*High maintenance*" is all I could think. When she excused herself to use the restroom, Paul looked at me with the "So what do you think?" look.

I replied, "Dude, what's up? She cut her motz stick with a fork and knife, what kind of diva is she?"

This was so much more than simply a bro code type thing. I was honestly concerned for my friend. There are many ways I've described Paul in my life, but dainty has never been one. Paul is a throw-a-steak-on-the-grill-and-eat-it-with-bare-hands-after-we-played-ball type of guy. So, someone as refined as Dani, cutting finger food with a knife, had me worried. Had she made him go so soft that he didn't even notice? Was he going to quit eating Whataburger next?

Paul cracked up as she walked back to our booth and said, "Ask her."

Dani replied, "Ask her what?"

I was trapped. I had to man up and ask her why she was such a diva. Paul was laughing, and Tricia was hanging her head in shame because she realized she was married to, "That Guy."

As Dani sat down, I said "So, you cut your Mozzarella Sticks..."

Paul laughed and I heard Dani tell this story for the first time.

Dani: Paul and Henry had taken the time to cultivate a relationship where they could be deeply honest with one another. Henry could be truthful and hold a mirror to Paul for a serious

relationship he was in. Having just met me, Henry and I had not yet invested the time it takes to create that kind of trust.

Investing the time and taking risks with people you trust allows you to speak deeper meaning into their story.

Henry: It's full disclosure time. I've struggled with spelling my entire life. When I say entire life, I mean it. As a child I was diagnosed with dyslexia and dysgraphia. If it hadn't been for my wife, proofreading my papers, I would have flunked out of graduate school. Throughout the planning of this book, I switched "pear" and "pair" constantly. I would draw a picture of the fruit and write "pair" underneath it. I know there were times that Dani was frustrated with me and my bad spelling. But, my bad spelling helped me realize something:

pears need pairs and pairs need pears

Allow me to explain. We all want to live fruitful lives. There is something deep in us that longs for that "more" in our story. Every culture tells stories that inspire people toward something greater; something that bears fruit. For me "pear" is the hook for this concept. It gives me a place to hang the end goal because it is easy to forget that the only way you'll see fruit is if you live in community with others. See, pears need pairs.

When we don't see fruit from our relationships we give up on them. We have such a longing for the "more" because pairs need pears.

If we are honest, there are some pairs that are just more fruitful than others. Some people draw the story out of us when one doesn't seem evident. At some tables the conversation is just more fruitful.

When we look to nature—to actual fruit—there is no way to fully predict which seed will grow or how much one will produce. There are some things though that set up a more fruitful environment: good soil, water, and plenty of sun, to name just a few. In the

same way, there are some things that set up relationships to be fruitful; to tell *more than a story*. The water, soil, and sun of fruitful relationships are truth, respect, understanding, support, and time; or what I call T.R.U.S.T.[1]

Dani: We desire to live fully and honestly in a Jerusalem community where we can authentically be who we are. A place where we are accepted as a whole person, and not just for the good we offer. To establish those types of relationships, people need time together. Time that helps build the type of trust which allows us to be vulnerable and take risks of speaking truth into each other's life. Time spent in relationships allows us to see the choices people make. It gives us the opportunity to be a part of their thoughts and opinions regarding other people, culture, religion, politics, and life. You have the opportunity with time to measure the weight of their words against their actions.

Henry: The bookend T's of T.R.U.S.T. are Truth and Time. Just like some relationships are more fruitful that others, some things just stick better. The sticky factor is why I like attaching words to images; it's also why I like acrostics and mnemonics. If you were sitting in the coffee shop[2] with me I wouldn't just tell you about T.R.U.S.T, I'd steal a bar napkin and write it down.

If we want relationships that bear fruit, we need to invest our time in them, but we can't do it haphazardly. We invest in the things that have borne fruit in the past. The first way we start investing is by telling the truth.

Dani: I can tell you without hesitation one person I count on to tell me the truth, no matter what. It is my mother. She is a faith-driven woman who values truth above all else. I have spent my whole life near her, talking with her, doing life together with her. Thus, I know that she doesn't just value truth—she lives for it. For that reason I know that no matter what I ask, she will give me her honest opinion. She will speak truth to me. Due to the time spent

in that relationship, I know her opinions and lifestyle, which give credibility to her words and actions. I can trust her because she has proven to be trustworthy.

Henry: I have heard people say, "I'm not gonna lie" a lot more recently. I guess it's not really different than starting a statement with "honestly." Honestly, they both scare me a bit; I'm not gonna lie. I think this is the point Jesus is getting at when He says, "Let your yes be yes and your no be no, everything else is from Hell."[3] When I hear these phrases, I wonder, "Do you usually lie, but you are living so differently right now that it's worth a declaration?"

I have people that come into my office, perplexed and frustrated who say, "They just don't trust me."

When I was a youth director I thought this was something kids just said about parents. Now as a Pastor, I hear it from spouses and co-workers, teachers and bosses, entrepreneurs and lawn-care experts. When they say this, I always ask the same question, "Are you telling them the truth?"

If you are not, you will never have trust.

If you are, trust takes time.

Some of you might be thinking, "Man, this is so simple." If you were thinking that, you are totally right. But whatever you do, do not confuse simple and easy. T.R.U.S.T. is simple; but rarely, if ever, is it easy.

It is really important to note that truth goes beyond not lying. Sure, Dani's mom doesn't lie, but she also gives her honest opinion, even when she knows it would to be easier to withhold the truth. I'm amazed how many people will technically "not lie," but what they are telling is still far from the truth. They are hiding, and remember, hiding doesn't work.

Dani: Since we touched on hiding again, I want to address a deeper truth in this story and one of my biggest moments of

growth as a person. This truth is hard for me to admit and also to share. Vulnerability works against hiding and the idea of a false identity. It is also a sure way to gain trust. So I want to step into the vulnerability.

Within the days and weeks after the accident, I remember having an overwhelming feeling of thankfulness. Not only that, but I also now had a very strong awareness of myself. It was a time in my life where my physical appearance meant far more to me than my character. I was a girl caught up in the whirlwind of American teen pop culture, idolizing beauty and sexuality. It's embarrassing now to admit that my value came from compliments or how many people noticed me. I wish I could have been that confident person who learned from an early age to embrace who they were. I wish I had lived into that truth.

I would like to say that, but I can't, not in a chapter focused on truth. My story is one full of compliments on the way I looked. These slowly over time became who I was, or at least who I thought I was. If I wasn't appreciated for the way I looked, then who was I?

The season of life that takes you from adolescence into adulthood is filled with anxieties and questions of who you are as a person, who you want to be, and what makes you unique. It is a struggle to find those answers which surround your identity while living inside the social pressure to fit in.

I hid my insecurities and questions, my mistakes and doubts behind the makeup I wore to be accepted. My false identity kept me from discovering who I really was. Being a young adult, it is easy to feel lost and confused, while giving the impression of confidence. This tension creates a disconnect within ourselves and it tears at our spirit. Eventually, if self discovery and acceptance of who we are doesn't happen at a young age, we continue to hide behind a persona well into adulthood. This will create major problems later on. The longer you hide, the harder it is to figure out

who you really are.

My false self was formed by the propaganda I created with make-up, clothes, and the people I spent time with. The way I behaved stemmed from that foundation. To belong with the beautiful people, I played the part. I lived the lie that the way I looked was the only version of me that existed. I believed at the very least, it was the most important version of me and it was the reason I belonged.

Having my face smashed into a jet ski and then lying in bed for the next few days to recover, gave me a few hours to ponder what really is important. It could have all turned out so differently.

What if I had died?

What if I was disabled?

What if I was permanently disfigured?

What if I never looked the same and my new face was worse than the one I knew?

What if I had broken my shoulder and couldn't dance or play softball or be in the school play?

What if there was internal damage and I couldn't have children?

"What ifs" can make a person go crazy if we continually fixate on them. Taking a small amount of time, however, to really let the weight of those words settle in after a life altering moment can help you take inventory of the important things in life. We must give the "what ifs" space to deepen our understanding, yet not allow them to exist outside their rightful place. Outside that space, these words become a weapon to keep you disappointed and fearful. They prevent you from moving forward with your life.

Allowing time to process the "what ifs" in those couple days helped me to re-evaluate my priorities. The accident revealed to me how one small moment can change everything in your life. I was spending my time creating a complex and superficial false identity.

God used that moment to reveal to me that I was more than I was willing to see. I didn't understand and appreciate who I was inside of my own skin. I didn't see that my life meant more and could be more than just trying to win the social popularity contest. I was more than just skin deep, and I owed it to myself and the people around me to allow them into my real identity.

Henry: Did you feel that?

I remember the first time Dani and I were preparing for a talk and she shared that part of the story; that truth with me. I remember what I felt—it was a deep respect. We have all had moments like Dani described, but when someone is brave enough to be vulnerable and tell that truth, respect is the fruit.

Trust can be destroyed in a moment with a lie or revealed deception, but it takes time to build. When someone tells the truth consistently, over a long period of time, they will earn respect.

Do the guys on the team respect me?

Does my girlfriend's dad respect me?

Does my employer respect me?

As a child, I cannot remember how many times my mother told me, "Do not lie to me. If you lie the punishment will be worse. If you tell the truth you will get in less trouble."

It is childish to think that if I tell the truth, I will not get in trouble. As an adult, telling the truth is about ownership. It's about earning respect from others and even oneself. Coach K4 recalls a time during his freshman year at West Point when he was running late and walked through the lawn getting his shoes dirty. Shoes were not allowed to be dirty or scuffed at West Point, but must always gleam from their spit shine. When some upperclassmen stopped him to inspect his uniform and asked him why his shoes were dirty, the only allowed response was, "No excuse sir."

There is a reason such a successful man recalls that moment. This

reality can be summarized in a status update that came across my Facebook feed the other day:

Own your baggage, or it will own you.
Deal with it, or it will deal with you.

It does not matter if it's dirt on your shoe, insecurities, or disfigurement; when we own the truth, we earn respect. When we don't own the truth, it always comes back to bite us. I have seen people try all kinds of things to get respect; but the reality is, respect is the effect of telling the truth over time.

Dani: Yes, respect is the fruit of telling the truth over time, however, there are and always will be people who will not understand. A few years ago I told my story of crashing my face into a jet ski at a youth conference. Once I came off stage, an eager 12- year-old boy came up to me and said, "I couldn't see it before, but I can totally see the disfigurement in your face up close."

"Um…What?" I held my tongue and silenced a sarcastic comment. Since I'm a professional, I looked politely at the young boy and said, "I don't know if you heard me, but I'm OK. There is nothing wrong with me now. I look just like I did before the accident. This is just my face."

At that point he put his hand on my shoulder, shook his head, and said matter-of-factly, "No, no, no…It's ok. It's not that bad."

I shook my head and replied, "Thank you."

You will choose to be vulnerable.

You will choose to share your story.

But, there will always be some people like the young boy at the conference who, even when hearing the truth laid out before them, will walk away not understanding. There will also be people who just don't understand at first. They see what they want to see and then pass judgment. Henry saw a girl too proud to touch her food with her fingers. It is only after having a conversation that is based

on respect that understanding is found. At supper that evening, so many years ago, we talked about my accident. Henry then understood me and better understood why Paul wasn't put off by my momentary high maintenance needs. He knew that two weeks after that dinner I was receiving my permanent teeth. The dentist recommended that I be extra careful not to break my temporary retainer until my scheduled surgery, which is why I was careful not to bite into my food.

As storytellers, we are responsible to the story within us and the truth and richness that we have found. We have the opportunity to share the way that God has revealed himself to us through the experiences of our lives. What we cannot control is how and when our story will impact other people. We can only be faithful to sharing our lives with others in hopes of having conversations that bear fruit. When it doesn't, we can simply enjoy a fun story and walk away.

Henry: It was tough for me to understand that walking away is part of respecting the truth of the story. But understanding is exactly what respect, lived in over time, produces. Respect earned by telling the truth over time can be confused with getting off the hook, just like some may confuse understanding with agreement. If I tell the truth to someone who disagrees, or has a different truth than I do, this doesn't mean they will agree with me. There are some relationships that have high degrees of respect built on years of individuals speaking the truth to each other, with very little agreement. It does not matter how much you love or care about another person, you will not always agree with them and they will not always agree with you. However, understanding is still very achievable and pairs that live in understanding can still be highly fruitful.

Dani: Henry mentioned that understanding and agreement are not the same thing. It is so easy for us to interchange these ideas when really they are so different. It often feels that agreement has to be

found in order for there to be peace. Agreement often leads to the idea that there is a right and wrong way. When we have people who agree with us, then we feel justified in the way we think and live. It then becomes very easy to surround ourselves with like-minded people—people, who live the same way, think the same way, and agree with our belief system. I would consider this comfortable living.

I understand the benefit in this philosophy. It is encouraging and uplifting to be with people who support your lifestyle. One problem, however is that the people who are so much like us, tend to have the same blind spots that we do. The dark side is when we then grow uneasy and fearful of anyone or anything outside our lifestyle system. I have often noticed that when we don't understand something, we become afraid of it and it settles into a stereotype. It lives in a box that we can gauge and judge and keep at a safe distance, far away from our comfort. The gift in having life experiences with people not like you is how much they push at your ideas, thoughts, emotions, and lifestyle. It creates space for you to have conversations with people who give you a new perspective. When new ideas are pushed up against your belief system, it gives you the chance to wrestle with what you truly believe. It brings our own blind spots into clear view. Then in the end, you don't have to agree. We must guard against isolation, for sometimes there is no right or wrong, but an understanding that you both do things differently. There is so much respect in these relationships because you know that it is based in truth. These people won't just tell you what you want to hear. You can trust what they say. They help shape your life in a way that no other relationship can, because it forces you to actively participate in your thoughts, beliefs, and lifestyle.

Henry: Sometimes you'll have to work really hard to grow T.R.U.S.T. Like everything, truth took time to blossom into respect, respect must be lived in for a season before understanding buds, and this may take years to grow into support. In T.R.U.S.T, each

concept is the fruit of the concept before it. It was because Paul and I had filled a treasure chest of T.R.U.S.T. that he introduced me to Dani for the first time.

Dani: Telling the truth over time. It earns you respect. Vulnerability, being able to be honest even when it's hard, sharing your honest opinion and working towards understanding, even with people you disagree with breaks down barriers and creates communities. These relationships are imperative to finding hidden meaning in the stories of your life, and refining who you are.

CHAPTER 5:

I Kicked a Dog

~by Henry

"See, what had happened was…"

This is never a good way to start a story. It's a weasel line and everybody knows it. The person that says it knows they are trying to get out of something. The person hearing it knows that what follows is going to be a weak attempt at an excuse or the beginning of a tall tale. It falls in the category of, "The fish was this big…"

Yet, those are the exact words that came out of my mouth when I was doing the yearlong internship required by my tribe, to become a pastor. My boss walked into my office with an interesting look on his face.

"Vicar," that's the title they give to the intern, "I hear you've been walking around kicking dogs."

My assignment was to a church in Southern California that has a preschool and a grade school attached to it. One of the teachers made a special trip to share with the pastor her concern about something she heard. In my experience, when this happens it is usually in reference to some dark stuff, like a child having cancer or suspected abuse. News has to be pretty important to pull a teacher away from her break or classroom prep. What she heard my daughter Adeline say was just that frightening,

> My dad kicked that dog so hard that he probably broke its
> ribs. It was like when he kicks a soccer ball. That dog flew
> so far, and yelped so loud, and I was so scared.

Even as I write these words, I understand the teacher's concern. Pastor already knew my character, but he was also my boss, and as such had to follow up on these kinds of accusations.

That's when it happened. Pastor confronted me, and "See, what happened was…" came out of my mouth.

Before I can tell you what I told my boss, you deserve a little background information. Since my girls were very little we have had what we call "Daddy/Daughter Dates." What we do and when

we do it changes over the years. From the time my oldest, Kaitlyn, was in preschool until around second or third grade, we went to Starbucks every Tuesday morning before school. The kids hot chocolate was only a buck, so it was something we could do each and every week.

"I would like a kids hot chocolate at 100 degrees, please." That was her opening line. Kaitlyn was so articulate and specific, that every employee quickly learned her name and a lot about her. They knew that her favorite subjects were art and math. They knew the chapter of the book that mom had read to her the night before. They knew what the plans for the playground were that day.

She also told them all about me. They knew I was in graduate school, studying communication. They knew I worked at a church and spoke all over the world. They knew when I ran a yellow light and the officer let me off with a warning (he was a regular too). So, the day that I booked a half dozen speaking gigs with one organization, sure enough that Tuesday the Starbucks staff knew my Spring Schedule. When Kaitlyn mentioned Seattle, Washington as one of my destinations, one of the staff members explained that Starbucks was started in Seattle. When we sat down Kaitlyn looked at me and said, "Daddy, since we come here every week for our Daddy/Daughter date, it would only seem appropriate that we visit the company's place of origin together. What do you think?"

Who could argue with that? She was only eight years old and was just so articulate and quick on her feet that I couldn't counter her argument. So she joined me for my gig in Seattle and we had our fanciest Daddy/Daughter Date yet—dinner at the top of the Space Needle.

She ordered the grilled cheese and fries.

What we do on our Daddy/Daughter Dates varies from 45 minutes, one dollar hot chocolate to flying across the country for a weekend. What we do however, will never be as important as the time we

spend together.

That's a good thing because money was incredibly tight on my internship that even the dollar for Starbucks wasn't in the budget. So we switched it up. That year, every morning before school my younger daughter Adeline and I would walk our dog Coco together. We would walk, and talk, and laugh.

Kids think differently than adults and although it cost no money, she saw a daily Daddy/Daughter date as an upgrade. I didn't know at the time how many memories, especially this one, were being created.

One of the things I've always done, especially during Daddy/Daughter Dates is look for teachable moments. Even though Adeline was only 6 years old, I knew that learning to walk the dog herself would teach her a lot. By walking a dog, any child would learn: confidence, critical thinking, the balance between being strong and gentle, leadership skills...the list could go on, but you get the idea.

This year was different.

We were an Indiana family living in Southern California for a year. Not only that, but we were ethnic minorities for the first time in our lives. We were the only Anglos, (that's the way white people are referred to when they are the minority in a predominantly Hispanic area), on our block. In the seven blocks where we would walk Coco, there were only a few non-Hispanic families. So our dog walking was also a cross-cultural immersion experience.

One of the first things we realized living there was that people lived in very close quarters with large extended families. The four of us felt cramped in our two bedroom, one bathroom, 600 square foot side of the duplex. This was the first time my daughters had shared a bedroom. Yet, all of our neighbors lived as extended family. On the other side of the wall that connected our homes, Mom and Dad had their 3 children, as well as Dad's brothers, and their wives, and children, and even grandma. There were 16 people living on the

other side of the duplex.

We were in a different world.

My wife and daughters quickly realized that gender roles were also lived out very differently from the white culture we had been used to. Adeline, loving animals of all shapes and sizes, also realized that the way the neighbor treated animals was different. No one, except our family, kept their dog on a leash. In fact, no one except our family took their dog for a walk; they just let the dogs out at night. Tricia and I would joke that the dogs were running in gangs at night and we wondered if Disney had visited this neighborhood for inspiration when writing Lady and the Tramp.

On our Daddy/Daughter Date walks, Adeline and I talked about all these things, especially the way people treated animals. During the day, only the little dogs would wander the streets. The bigger dogs—leaders of the gangs we imagined—were inside fenced yards. Often these dogs would bark and frighten both Coco and Adeline. So, I taught Adeline to think ahead and plan. She knew the house where the big grey dog would run the fence, growling and barking while we were on the adjacent sidewalk. I asked her what we could do before we got there. She decided it was best to cross the street. This was a good choice and I let her know that.

The house directly across the street had a rickety wooden six-foot privacy fence. They also had one of the loudest dogs in the neighborhood. On one end it would stick its snout under the fence, just past a shrub, and still find a way to bark loudly. At the other end, it would jump on top of the trash cans on every day except Monday. Monday was trash day and the cans were by the side of the street. It would bark, and yelp, and jump so we could see its snarling sharp teeth. We had to walk by this house both as we left on our walk, and as we came back. Because of this I taught her about bravery and the way it affected others. I'd tell her, "Bravery isn't the absence of fear; it is acting in spite of fear."

Then after the dog would growl we'd talk about how she felt. She realized if she acted brave and kept walking confidently, Coco wouldn't be as scared. One day she told me it was the same with the kids on the playground. If she was brave and tried something new, other kids would too. While this has led to multiple broken bones, I count them as a small investment in bravery.

It was a great morning when, after passing that house with the grey dog, Adeline said, "All bark and no bite, that's what that dog is."

She had heard the phrase on a TV show and put together what it meant on her own. We talked about that concept for the next couple of weeks. We might still be talking about it if we hadn't realized this dog was indeed both bark and bite.

As we were walking across our street, the dog jumped up on the trash cans and began its customary growl. That morning, as its full body weight slammed against the fence, the fence finally couldn't hold it. In a single push, the boards cracked then shattered as the salivating beast exploded through the fence. As it leapt toward us with its matted black fur and terror filled eyes, Adeline didn't know what to do with Coco, so she froze. Coco, a 15 pound Pomeranian fur ball, who thinks she is the toughest dog around, jaunted toward the other dog in attack mode, putting herself between the dog and Adeline.

As Adeline froze everything went into slow motion for me.

I saw the jaws of this dog open, as it took one step, then two, and on the third leapt into the air. I did not know if this beast would take a bite out of my daughter, maiming her body, or aim for our dog, breaking Adeline's heart.

I stepped forward with my right foot then planted my left. A decade of dormant muscle memory awoke with a single clean sweep as I connected with the dog the same way I had during years of goalie kicks. Just as I had cleared the ball downfield defending my net, I had cleared the dog, defending my daughter.

Placing myself between the now angered dog and my daughter, I was ready for round two. My eyes were locked on the beast, and this was a stare down I refused to lose. Feeling Adeline had her wits about her and knowing our house was within sight, I asked, "Can you get Coco home safely?"

She boldly exclaimed, "I won't let anything happen to her, Daddy!"

I stood, eyes locked with the dog for what seemed much longer than it was. Adrenaline has that effect. It also makes you think you can do things you otherwise wouldn't attempt. Eventually the dog ran off and I went up to my neighbor's door. They were getting ready to go to work and school, but I thought it was essential they know what had happened, even if it was just to cover myself from any liability. I had no idea if I had hurt their dog. I didn't know if my neighbors would attempt to sue me. Another part of me just wanted them to catch their dog and fix their fence so that this wouldn't happen to anyone else.

All kinds of emotions, thoughts, and scenarios rushed through my head as I walked up to the door. Yet, not a single scenario included the reality that I did not speak Spanish and that they did not speak English. I tried to tell them what had happened and in frustration ended up pointing to the fence, growling with a vain attempt at pantomime. To this day, I don't know if they know what happened. They may be telling a different story of the loco gringo who kicked their fence letting their dog out and then came and growled at the door.

I know my daughter hadn't processed it that morning. Nor had she when she explained what had happened on our morning walk, standing a few feet away from the preschool fence.

So here's the point. The moral of the story, if you will:

> There will always be attacks from enemies
> (usually at the most inopportune times),
> yet there will always be protection and provision…
> even if we don't always see it.

But there's more than a moral…

Dani: As I read this story, one thing I enjoyed seeing was the relationship of Henry with his daughters. There are countless hours of investment there. I know Henry, and his children are a priority in his life. Spending time with his girls, learning about them, and winning their hearts are very important pieces in his relationship with them. He wants to be with them because he loves them. He rejoices over them and he wants to know them more deeply.

He also desires for them to know him. To have a true relationship, spending time together allows you to know things about each other, deepening love and building T.R.U.S.T. This is the foundation for their relationship.

I mention this because for Adeline, something very scary had happened to her. Not only the life of her small dog, but also her life felt in jeopardy. For this moment, there was no escape, only the threat and reality of being hurt beyond her understanding. Something very terrifying was coming straight toward her. Her skills and ability couldn't get her out of this. She was, however, with someone who could protect her, someone who could help her and fight the enemy for her.

It reminds me of an afternoon when I was a young girl. My sister and I spent countless hours playing at a friend's home. Her parents had converted their whole attic into a full-blown playroom. After we had worn every costume and pretended to be every character in every story we knew, we went outside to play. While we were chasing each other in a game of tag, I ran down the street and passed a driveway where a man was washing his car. This stood out

to me because he was so focused on his car that he forgot to close his gate to keep his extra large chocolate lab from running away.

The dog immediately saw us running and ran after us. Never having had a pet, I didn't understand that this animal wanted to play. As a five year old, I only saw a dog as big as me, chasing me down the street, convinced he was out to attack me. My sister and my friend were older than me, and admittedly faster, so they made it safely inside the house.

I wasn't so lucky.

The large chocolate lab ran straight toward me and jumped on top of me. I fell to the ground and tucked myself in a ball. I was crying out for help and was scared as this dog proceeded to put his mouth on me, nipping and biting trying to get my attention. He was pouncing on me and nudging me to get up. When the owner finally caught up with us, he took hold of his dog. That is when he noticed that my knees were bitten deep and scraped up. I laid there on the sidewalk, waiting while the owner took his dog back home and put him behind the fence. He came back and carried me to my friend's home where her mother cleaned me up, and wrapped my knees, offering relief from the pain.

I had a similar experience to Adeline who was confronted with something incredibly scary. I just didn't have someone there to protect me.

Henry: As we tell our story, and listen to others, we are each drawing from a different well of experience. Some stories will resonate, while others will be met with resistance. A story of protection may evoke a knowing peace, vengeful animosity, or a plethora of other options. But, you see, it is conversation that moves a story to something deeper and richer. Around the table, we must learn how to listen to the stories of descent that may be stirred up in others. By doing this, it gives us new perspectives, greater understanding, and deeper compassion.

Over the last couple months I've been teaching my oldest daughter Kaitlyn to drive. As I've been teaching her, many stories of my learning to drive have surfaced. One month and one day after my sixteenth birthday I took my driving test for the first time. That was the earliest you could take the test in those days and I was there as soon as school let out. Having already passed the written test I told all my friends I was going to the DMV to pick up my driver's license after school. I'll admit that was a bit cocky, but that is who I was back then.

I parked on the right hand side of the street in the parking space closest to the stoplight. As the test began I put on my seatbelt, started the car, and held my hands at ten and two. I had learned how to time the lights and pull out into traffic downtown, so I was confident. The cross street light turned from green to yellow and I prepared for it to turn red. I knew that mine would then turn green. The mixture of excitement and nerves led me to take off a little too quickly when the light turned green. I was watching the lights change so closely that, in my haste, I didn't use my side-view mirror and see the oncoming car that was also timing the lights.

Fortunately, I took off so quickly that I was far enough in front of him and he didn't hit me. Unfortunately, failure to yield the right of way when entering in traffic equals failure of a driving test. So I had to attempt it again on April 20, two months and one day after my sixteenth birthday.

That was a very long month; but I learned an important lesson. I learned to use my side-view mirrors because I have huge blind spots. Other people's stories are the same way. We can use them to see a fuller picture of our own story.

Dani: It is interesting to think of a fuller story; something that is more than what we have already experienced. It would be right to assume that being in the moment where the story is created gives you the entirety of what that experience has to offer. However, that

leaves us with only one perspective. Once a story is shared, it lives outside of us.[1] People hear it, and they connect to pieces of it with either past experiences or current circumstances. It allows you, the story holder, to see beyond what you experienced and see what it looks like through someone else's eyes. It becomes a stronger story the next time you share it. Our stories need other people to help us see what we cannot.

In the musical "Wicked" there is a beautiful song near the end where Elphaba and Glinda are discussing their friendship and the importance of how they each have impacted one another. These words say it best,

> I've heard it said that people come into our lives for a reason, bringing something we must learn and we are led to those who help us most to grow if we let them and we help them in return. Well, I don't know if I believe that's true, but I know I'm who I am today because I knew you...It well may be that we will never meet again in this lifetime so let me say before we part, so much of me is made from what I learned from you. You'll be with me like a handprint on my heart and now whatever way our stories end, I know you have re-written mine by being my friend...Who can say if I've been changed for the better? But because I knew you, I have been changed for good.[2]

When I share my experience with Henry, as a response to his story, it changes the way he looks at that moment with Adeline. Revealing that dark memory in me was not his intention or how he thought it would impact me. Yet, my story gives his story a new understanding. When we share those moments, we hold the power to enlighten and learn from one another.

Moments full of light for us can evoke darkness in others. The reverse is the same as well. We live in a world that is a muddled mess of good and bad, right and wrong, healing and hurtful. It

is often stated that you can't have one without the other. To understand that you have light, you must experience darkness. We live in a sinful world, and even while there are moments of pure joy, darkness still exists. Death, disease, sickness, natural disaster, war, and corrupt politics each have a way of effecting of us. No one is exempt from these things. Age, race, gender, or social status won't shield you from living life in the hard places. There are tough things in each of our lives that we must navigate through.

Jesus said that "The thief comes only to steal and kill and destroy; but, I have come that they may have life, and have it to the fullest."[3] We each have experienced the thief coming but we must not forget Jesus' "but". He brings life in the very midst of the thief coming to steal, kill, and destroy.

Full life is knowing who you are and whose you are. It is not ignoring the weakness and brokenness, but embracing it completely in a full understanding of what God designed in you. Knowing you belong to God allows you to trust in His love and mercy. Together, these two create an identity that frees you to participate fully in life.

Henry: The story started very simply. Not the story in this chapter but our story as people. God's role was to protect and provide what He had created. In fact, one of the ways He did this was by telling Adam and Eve not to eat from a certain tree. People had a role too. We were to unpack creation; organize it and make it grow. When Adam and Eve disregarded these roles, it unleashed all kinds of bull. However, I never see that God took away the basic plot. I haven't found anywhere in the Bible where God says my job is no longer to protect and provide for you. Likewise, I don't see anywhere where our responsibility to be fruitful and multiply, unpacking and organizing creation is taken away. The problem is, sometimes the story we tell misses the point completely. Sometimes it flips the plot.

What Adeline's teacher overheard that day was bad, it missed

the plot. It probably isn't as bad as the story in which one girl attempted to settle an argument between a group of her friends. In a classic "My Dad is tougher than your Dad" scenario, the first child had said, "If you don't stop, I'm going to call my dad, he's a cop and he'll arrest you."

The little girl she was playing with had even less of a grasp on her father's vocation and replied, "Well my dad's a firefighter and if you do, I'll call him and he'll burn your house down."

All of this escalated when the Pastor's daughter who was very proud of her dad—but like many young girls attributed much more authority and power to his job than it really had—replied, "If you two don't stop, I'm calling my dad. He's a Pastor, and he'll send you Hell."

We all have a way of missing the point.

Dani: We often only see what we want to see, or hear what we want to hear. My struggle, as my husband informs me, is that I have selective listening, and he's right. I remember my Aunt Barb saying to me, "It's so important to have other people who can help you see what you can't see because you are too close to your own story." However, too often, we end up missing not only the point or lesson we need to learn, but we deprive others from hearing the truth that changed our life.

Henry said, "The problem is, sometimes the story we tell misses the point completely." Sometimes the story I tell has a way of making me look better. We bloat our ego and miss the opportunity to admit weakness.

For Adeline, her dad single-handedly took on a huge dog and was fearless as he kicked it to protect his daughter. For Henry, it was a reminder of not only God's original plan to protect his people, but his call for us to protect others. Adeline's is a fun story to tell, and her dad looks really cool in her version. Henry's version speaks to a deeper meaning that calls to our inmost need to be protected by

God and for this protection to overflow in our helping to protect others. That day, Adeline missed the greatness of the story, but that is why we share our lives with others, to reveal its truth.

Henry: Dani and I are not just encouraging you to come to the table, enter into conversations, and discover you are living more than a story; we strive to do it as well. As we have, there are some big questions that even the most seasoned pastors and profound professors struggle to answer. As we talk about protection; we would be remiss if we ignore the elephant in the room.

What happens if God isn't protecting us? He allows pain, and natural disasters, and all kinds of other evil. There are very good people that have very bad things happen to them, while wicked people seem to prosper. Why is this?

First, I want to acknowledge how big these questions are. I've tossed and turned and lost sleep over them. I've wondered if they are just too big to tackle. Yet, while just ignoring them would be easier, it would continue to miss the plot.

I'm professionally a Pastor,[4] but before that I was a professor and there is a huge difference between the two. As a professor, I would ponder these types of philosophical questions. While this has its place; these are conversations best reserved for a pub. As a Pastor, I've held the hands of a weeping widow who happened to be a very good person who had a very bad thing happen to her. It is there I learned that all my professorial pondering had no place in this moment. Like every table, mine is filled with people who have endured sorrow, despair, cancer, and acts of abuse (physical, emotional, sexual, and verbal). At times individuals lose homes and jobs, spouses and children. This bull is part of the story.

These tough questions that have tougher answers—if any answers at all—are a part of our story.

But, it's all about the story, isn't it?

His story.

Her story.

Their story.

Our story.

Sometimes his story of protection and provision will stir up her story of fear. But, together they may discover more than a story.

They may discover a parable.

Dani: We believe our soul longs for these parables. We desire to share our story and to be heard. We long to share our pain and our joy. We want not only to hear, but to live better stories.

Heavenly stories that reach far beyond ourselves.

Stories of fruitfulness.

But you can't live a parable without owning the bull.

CHAPTER 6:

The Baby Whisperer

~by Dani

We all know someone who just seems to be a target for mistreatment or heartache. Who knows, maybe you are that person. That person in my life is my sister. The only thing worse than experiencing beat down after beat down is watching someone you love go through it over, and over, and over, and over again. My sister is one of the kindest and softest souls to walk the earth. And yet, she is an incredibly courageous person because she chooses to get out of bed every day and face life. Sometimes that alone will qualify you among the strong and brave.

My sister Kelly has a great love for children and has been a nanny for countless years. In fact, I am not sure I have ever seen her not holding a baby or going off to babysit for a friend. She is the baby whisperer. It's fun to watch her and see how children respond to her. She truly has a gift.

Six years ago she just started a new job as the nanny on the overnight shift to 8-week-old premature twin boys. Both babies had acid reflux so they had to be fed only 1-2 oz of a special formula every couple hours. This family had two nannies for 24-hour around the clock assistance. Kelly would get to work at 10 each night, and start her shift with cleaning and chores until midnight when she would feed the babies.

After feeding and burping the babies separately, one of them started fussing. Kelly picked him up and he threw up all over. She turned him over on her arm so he was on his tummy (this position calms an upset stomach for infants). He then stopped crying and she thought he was OK. Then, all of a sudden, as he laid on her arm, his whole body got heavy and went limp.

She turned him over and saw his lips turning blue. It appeared like he was swallowing his tongue. The parents were in the house and because they had been in the hospital before for something similar, she quickly went to go get them.

Going up the stairs with both babies, Kelly called out for their mom. When their mom woke up she took her baby, put him over her shoulder, and started rubbing his back. Kelly continued to tell her the baby wasn't breathing. The mom dialed 911 as Kelly started CPR until the EMS got there and took over. Knowing these children had been through so much, and hoping for the best, Kelly tended to the other baby until the day nanny arrived. As they changed shifts, the day nanny shared with Kelly that the baby had a similar episode less than a month earlier.

Not even 24 hours after the baby had been in the hospital, the father and the day nanny accused Kelly of causing Shaken Baby Syndrome.

My father, who has been a Police officer, evidence inspector, and for the last five years of his career, a Sergeant Detective could immediately recognize multiple red flags. The father, who was scared, continued to throw blame Kelly's way. Since my father knew Kelly's rights and wanted to help protect her, he made sure she said nothing. Child Protective Services contacted my family a week after the incident. My dad hired an attorney and kept Kelly from being questioned until there was an actual case against her, and then the baby passed away.

Talking with my sister during that time, I could hear the heart wrenching pain in her voice. So many times she couldn't even finish her sentences due to the tears that wouldn't stop coming. I lived 12 hours away, and I could do nothing. I could hear her absolute desperation of losing a baby that was in her care.

A baby that was small and innocent and sick.

A baby whom she loved.

Kelly did what we all do, replaying those moments over and over in our mind, questioning her actions and timeline to make sure she hadn't done something wrong. There was a baby who died and her heart was broken.

After eight months of hearing nothing, my family's attorney contacted my father and informed him that Kelly would be charged with first degree murder and first degree child abuse.

My kind and gentle hearted sister was facing the potential of life in prison, if convicted. I couldn't believe what was happening.

When my dad called to tell me, my knees got weak and I collapsed to the ground. I dropped the phone to the floor and my head in my hands.

I couldn't focus.

I couldn't think.

I couldn't see anything through the tears.

I could only see images of my soft spoken, kind hearted sister being put in handcuffs and hauled away to a jail cell. We've all seen the movies. My thoughts and feelings were overwhelming. I couldn't grab any one thought to hold on to. This couldn't be right. It had to be a mistake. How is she going to get through this? I must have heard wrong.

My sister...

    going to jail...

        for life...

            for the murder of a sick infant.

Paul took the phone, and he talked with my dad as I curled up on his lap. My father explained that because he, my mom, Paul, and I were going down to Haiti in less than five hours, the prosecutor arranged for Kelly to turn herself in after we got back from Haiti one week later. It was decided that mom would stay back with Kelly because she was so scared and fragile while the three of us would lead the mission team, as best we could.

The following week when we returned, Kelly was set up to go before the judge for her arraignment on the charges. More than 60 people showed up to support her. Before entering the courtroom, my uncle prayed with everyone present, which took the prosecutor by surprise who had never, in his 35 years of practicing law, seen anything like that. Friends, family, people whom Kelly had worked with and hadn't seen in years were all there to support her.

When she was asked if she was scared facing life in prison, Kelly responded, "I know God is going to get me through this. He is with me. I have never hurt a baby, and the truth will all come out." Even facing life in prison, she held onto her faith. I never realized how strong she was, and wondered if I could say the same.

With the courtroom full and tensions high, the judge heard both sides and set bail at $100,000. When my dad left the courtroom he wondered where he was going to get that much money. Friends and family came to him, writing checks and dipping into their life savings to assist in getting Kelly out. With their help and a deal with a bails bondsman, eight hours later, my dad was able to get his daughter out of jail.

During those eight hours, Kelly was handcuffed and put in a cell with another young girl. In Kelly's words, it was a spiritual battle. It was hours of wrestling against doubt and fear and failure. Hours of trying to hold onto the truth. She would remind herself that she was a child of God and the truth would come out. She knew God would see her through this because she belonged to Him.

Kelly would be under house arrest until the trial. She would wear an ankle bracelet and could only leave home from nine in the morning to five in the evening each day. Kelly was also not allowed to be near any children under the age of 18.

Through the next three months, Kelly's face and name appeared on the news. Things such as, "You had better watch out who you get to care for your children; local nanny to stand trial for mishandling an infant that resulted in death" were being said with her picture next to the headline. She was being treated as a guilty party before she

even went to trial. People would remember her name and face with this story. She couldn't get a job due to the publicity. She had bills to pay and no way to pay them.

This was one of the darkest times in Kelly's life. Depression would overwhelm her to the point of not being able to get out of bed. She has told me that she watched how God took care of her by sending people to her always at just the right moment when she needed it the most. Friends and family would come and share lunch with her. People would show up with a check for her rent, or for groceries. She had friends ordering homemade cards, or offering cleaning jobs to help provide an income. Family would come and take Kelly out for a meal or a walk, or to church. They were there to remind her she wasn't alone. My father will talk about how money would keep coming in to help pay for the attorney costs. The body of Christ showed up during this time. They prayed and prayed and prayed. They gave and they helped and they showed up.

My family's needs were not just met during this time, they were exceeded. After three months of working on her case, my father received a call that the case was dropped. Not only did they not have enough evidence to convict Kelly, but there wasn't even enough to stand trial.

The attorney said that he had never seen a murder case dropped before the trial. He also said he had never witnessed faith like my sister's, and my father's, and my mother's. Never had he experienced a community of people supporting someone like he had with my family.

The case was dropped.

The charges cleared.

Kelly was free.

So here's the point. The moral of the story, if you will:

Light shines brightest in the darkness.

But there's more than a moral...

Henry: I know the moral of this story is true, but I don't like the story.

I don't want to admit it's true.

Sure it has a good ending; but, I want to close my eyes and plug my ears because this reality just hurts too much.

When somebody asks what this book is about, I tell them "How a story can become more than a story." I tell them how it starts with "pair," the others we need to speak truth into our lives. As I've shared this part of the thesis, fun conversation filled with memories and laughter have happened on the spot. People talk about where they have seen this played out, telling me their story. I love to talk about "pairs" and the fruit that living *more than a story* brings.

But, when the conversation turns to the truth of bull, it all changes. Sometimes, we can laugh at someone else's silly bull. But I've yet to find someone who knows what to do in the midst of bull like Kelly and her family experienced.

I long to live *more than a story* and I know that without owning the bull, it is always something less. But such knowledge does not make it any more palatable. There are all kinds of ways we attempt to avoid and minimize the bull. This is a huge problem when you think about T.R.U.T.H.

Since language shapes culture, the very fact that this book would be significantly less marketable if we called it bull crap, tells me something about this culture. I can censor the language and write bull $#!*, but even with such censorship I can expect more than one chastising email. Don't get me wrong, I'm not advocating for profanity. The last thing I want is young kids running around with potty mouths. Yet, dirty things must be talked about, and dirty things sometimes need to be owned in their full filth. The very fact that we don't say dirty words, even when describing dirty things,

shapes the story we tell.

If I were writing in Greek, I wouldn't say bull; I'd say Skubala. Paul uses this word in Philippians 3:8, "For His sake I have suffered the loss of all things and count them as *skubala*, in order that I may gain Christ." Yet, I can't find an English Bible that accurately translates this word. While this certainly has its puritanical roots, I think it is a reflection of something even deeper. Simply, no one likes to tell the truth about the bull in its full filth because everyone wishes it wasn't there—or at least that it didn't have such a sharp sting.

I don't like Kelly's story because broken people, tragedy, and false accusations are far too real.

I don't like the *skubala*.

Dani: Stories like these still need to be heard. When I hear stories of great pain and loss where the person afflicted by such sorrow has this incredible faith and strength, I often wonder, would I be strong enough to endure what they did? Looking back on this story, I feel incapable. But the honest truth is, this entire experience was incredibly difficult for my sister, my parents, their friends, my grandparents, the church, the kids that Kelly babysits for, and even for us living so far away. In the midst of the pain, it is terribly...painful. This pain acts as a daily reminder of everything that had happened.

And so what do you hold on to? What gets you through each day? What is that thing that helps you get out of bed each morning and put one foot in front of the other? For me, it is knowing who I am.

Identity in its complete awareness and acceptance is fully lived out within the whole of a community. We discovered that the root word for clothing is the same root word for deception. That when we try to cover up and hide, we are in turn deceiving not only others, but also ourselves. This is revealed most clearly when lived in community. When we share our lives with others, we have two choices: own who we are, or pretend to be someone else. We live

in this tension of trying to run from the hard stuff hidden inside of us while longing to reveal our true selves. The reverse however, is what makes the community come alive and function together as it should. It is most often in the darkest moments, when we are at our most vulnerable, the most broken, and the most honest, that the community can be who they want and need to be. We as humans need a community to embrace us, to accept us, to guide and speak into our lives. It is in community that people share their darkness and their stories of heartache. Being vulnerable in this way helps heal the brokenness within ourselves. We were created to lean on each other in the most honest way possible.[1]

I am always surprised by the affirmation people receive when they share about their heartache and sadness within a community. You hear or read online people praising bloggers, activists, columnists, authors, "Thank you so much for being honest! It is so good to know I am not alone." Are we truly that hidden that such honesty would provoke such praise and admiration? Are individuals and communities so devoid of T.R.U.S.T. relationships that the basic truths are tantalizing? At our core we are craving acceptance within a community which calls for honesty and complete acceptance of oneself. By denying our true self, the community then can never be what it is meant to be.

Henry: One day I realized a Jewish friend would always refer to the stories of the Bible in first person. Even though it was 3500 years ago, long before my friend was born, he would say, "When we were slaves in Egypt." Being intrigued, I listened even more closely and noticed most of my Jewish friends said "we" when talking about the stories of Torah, rather than "they." So, one day, my friend said, "When we," and I rudely interrupted and asked, "Why do you do that?"

"Do what?" he responded, a bit taken back by my abrupt interrogation.

"You say 'we,' when you weren't there," I replied.

He looked at me and said, "You Christians don't get it, do you? Their story is my story; it is our story. We are a covenant people."

I liked that thought.

Their story is my story.

It is our story.

Kelly's story is my story.

It's real and gritty and it is mine. The fact that I don't like it has a lot more to do with my story, and hiding from it, then I want to admit. But the truth remains. Her story is my story. I too have been hurt and healed, accused and set free. So have you.

Dani: We spoke before about hiding who we are from people to try to fit within the community. The beauty in Kelly's story is there was no hiding. All the junk that Kelly was going through was put out there in the open and lived out within her community. Everything was exposed and even if she wanted to hide, Kelly couldn't. The lies that were being told were created to define her. To label her and turn her into something she wasn't: a murderer.

Yet, even though it was a daily struggle, and it was a very tough struggle, she continued to be who she was. I remember talking to Kelly during this time and she said to me, "I would never choose to go through this, but I realized today that I understand a little bit more what it must have felt like for Christ to stand before the angry mob and have them accuse him, calling him guilty and worthy of death when he was innocent. He stood there knowing the truth that he was the Son of God, and yet everyone called him guilty of things he didn't do. That just feels so much like me right now. His sacrifice means more to me now that I understand it better, because of this." Through this experience, Kelly was connected to her greatest source of peace, even though it was her hardest hour.

Henry: We've all had different experiences with the church. It is

about time we start owning all of these experiences because they are all of our stories. It wasn't until after I had served the church in a professional capacity for well over a decade that I started to understand the DNA of the Bible as covenant and kingdom.[2] As I've started to understand the Bible through this double helix, the tough verses that I'd previously ignored or explained away (like God asking Abraham to kill his son[3]) made sense.

One thing that many people don't realize is that our identity is given to us first, then we learn to live it out in obedience. When I perform a wedding and say, "I now pronounce you husband and wife," a new identity is given. The couple will learn to live this new identity but only after they have received it.

I was listening to an NPR interview the other day. A researcher had done a study on prostitutes, and interestingly enough, in this report each and every one of them recounted their father, or father figure, telling them they were a slut. One woman, hardened by a life of abuse, softened to a scared little girl as her voice trembled recounting the story. It was her first dance, and she spent the afternoon getting dressed up and doing her hair. Excited and innocent she bounded down the stairs to twirl for her father. He looked at her and said, "You look like a little slut." Her innocence and sexuality were shattered by those words. She went on to live into that false identity that her father had spoken into existence.

False identity is the key word in the last sentence. That young lady wasn't a slut. She was an innocent child. She was going to her first dance and hadn't even kissed a boy yet. Her father's words were spawned from the depth of Hell; but like all false accusations, they still held power.

Jesus tells us that "the thief," that is Satan himself, "comes only to kill, steal, and destroy."[4] One of the chief ways he does this is through speaking false identities to God's children. The only true identity we have is that covenant identity as God's children.

In the baptismal liturgy there is a little bit of an argument going on. If the child is too young to speak, I ask the parents, "How is this child to be named?" In the same way if the individual is able to speak, I ask them, "How are you to be named?" Then they answer with the name. My parents said "Henry John Graf V." This may seem innocent, but God rips even that false identity away. In baptism the identity of Henry was replaced by the name of the Father, Son, and the Holy Spirit.

Brokenness was replaced with wholeness.

I was given a new identity, a new name, and a community.

The thing that broke my heart when I heard that story on NPR is that this woman had lived out the false identity of slut that Satan[5] had spoken to her. The sad reality is that her story is my story. There are times when I too live into a false identity. For me it has never been prostitute, and my false identities of pastor and father, speaker and author, may seem more innocuous, but they really are the same bull. When Jesus said,

> But you are not to be called rabbi, for you have one teacher, and you are all brothers. And call no man your father on earth, for you have one Father, who is in heaven. Neither be called instructors, for you have one instructor, the Christ.[6]

A big part of what He was getting at was tearing way all deceptive identities. When I hear Kelly's story my heart breaks because Satan is still hurling a false identity. I weep at the *skubula* she and her family went through.

But her story is my story.

It is your story too.

Jesus prepared us for this when He said, "God is still with you when people insult you, persecute you, and falsely say all kinds of evil against you because of me."[7]

Dani: Imagine a room plunged in darkness. The blackness so thick you wouldn't be able to see your hand in front of your face. I love what lighting one candle does to a room like that. When one small light shines in the darkness, it no longer encompasses you; it doesn't cover you as it once did. You can see the glimmer and there is hope. Your soul starts to come alive again. Light pushes out darkness and gives you back life.

That is just the effect of one candle.

Each person is created with light that exists inside them. When we pretend to be someone or something other than who we truly are, that light doesn't shine. It can't, because we aren't being real or honest in who we are.

In this story we see Kelly living into her true identity, but one of the most beautiful pieces in this story is how the community surrounding my family lived out theirs. In the gospel of Matthew it says,

> You are the light of the world. A town built on a hill cannot be hidden. Neither do people light a lamp and put it under a bowl. Instead they put it on its stand, and it gives light to everyone in the house. In the same way, let your light shine before others, that they may see your good deeds and glorify your Father in heaven.[8]

There is something powerful when people come together as individuals living into their identity. Those lights then shine together.

Being confident and sure of who they were, this community lived out their identity by giving generously to someone else who needed it. They learned to live in T.R.U.S.T. relationships, and by doing so, shined brightly.

These stories inspire us because we see the more in the story.

The way it should be.

The way it could be.

At the end of my sister's story, the attorney sat speechless. Never had he witnessed such light in such a dark time. No one would argue that being falsely accused of murder of an infant is dark and heavy stuff. Facing life in prison is hell here on earth. Yet, the light shone brightly. It radiated and pierced hearts and lives. On these pages it continues its impact in the darkness of your heart, because this is your story too. We are drawn to the light; we crave it, we need it, it is our hope in the darkness.

CHAPTER 7:

Machetes and Madmen

~by Dani

When I lead mission teams to Haiti, we fill our time with building projects, visitations to Hospitals, helping out at orphanages and sightseeing around the city. This provides people with the opportunity to learn more about the culture, while also giving them a way to help and give back. A few days into the trip, it had been an exceptionally long day of building at the orphanage. We were piled on top of the equipment and each other for the long ride home through the streets of Port au Prince. We were covered in the dirt that comes from mixing mortar and hauling rock all day in the dusty foothills of the mountains. I sat up front in the passenger seat with my friend Drew and our driver Leonard.

On the very first trip I took to Haiti, Leonard was our driver. I will never forget the first time I saw his smile, greeting me more than 12 years ago.

No one could forget that smile.

Leonard's smile encompasses the entirety of his face, it radiates that brightly. His grin is only surpassed by his servant heart and great faith in the Lord. He gives and he serves for long hours every day as he drives us and many other mission teams. Over the years, Leonard has acquired a catchphrase that sums up his attitude, one that is uniquely his.

"No problem." Now imagine it with an amazing Caribbean twang.

He picks us up in the morning ready to take us to the work site. When we announce our plans have changed again, and he will be home much later than expected…

"No problem!"

At the work site we decide to leave early and head over to a hospital to do visitations, taking away his well-deserved break...

"No problem!"

Leonard greets us each morning with a sparkling clean bus that is full of gas and ready to go. The coolers are full of water and soda covered with fresh ice to get us through the heat. Each evening when he leaves us, he spends hours wiping down the dust and dirt, and prepares the bus for us for another day's work. He will go to such lengths as to drive a different route each day to keep us safe. Leonard would say to us, "I have been blessed by helping you today. It is good for my soul."

Throughout our ride back to the guesthouse, people were chatting in the back, telling stories from previous trips and lives back home. A few people gazed out the window watching the Haitian city life of street vendors and kids hanging around after school. With our limited Creole, Drew and I were asking Leonard all sorts of questions about Haiti and his family.

We approached a busy intersection, which did not have traffic lights. Traditionally, the cars and trucks trying to get through would inch forward, creating a traffic block. There is no way through or around the other cars, so we sat, like everyone else waiting in the same way.

I was laughing sharing a story with Leonard when I noticed a man walking directly next to the bright green bus we were in. He was angrily shouting in Creole, and while I couldn't understand a word he said, I could tell by his facial expressions he was furious. He yelled and screamed, searching the crowd for anyone to listen. As he came around the front of the bus we noticed his extra large, sharp metal machete glistening in the sun. He waved it back and forth screaming his outrage.

We sat quietly, eyes still fixed on this man, not wanting to draw attention to ourselves. Each one of us was wondering what he would do. Sitting next to Leonard, Drew leaned over and quietly asked him what the man was saying. Leonard hesitated and then responded, "It is better you not know."

Drew and I exchanged a quick sideways glance. We didn't take that as a good sign.

As he wove his way through the cars, this angry man stared straight at me. His eyes were full of rage and he wouldn't look away. He continued shouting and waving the machete above his head. He then came directly around the bus to the passenger side, where my arm remained casually draped out the window.

I was afraid to move.

I was afraid to look away.

I was afraid to breathe.

I just waited, wondering what he would do next.

His eyes were such a deep dark brown that they appeared black. Then he stopped screaming and looked at me, his gaze intense and probing. I continued to hold my breath.

Then as quickly as he appeared, he went away, searching for another audience.

I slowly exhaled, letting out a shaky breath. I realized I hadn't been breathing for the last few moments. I looked down and saw that I had grabbed Drew's hand; his fingers turning blue because I was squeezing so hard.

Drew, trying to lighten the very tense moment, turned to Leonard and said, "Hey Leonard, almost problem right?" playing on our friend's motto.

With a smile on his face, Leonard turned to Drew and without missing a beat, in his very next breath said, "OH NO! No problem! You die, you go see Jesus! It's a beautiful thing!"

I sat speechless.

I never once thought of seeing Jesus if death was what waited for me in that moment. I wasn't rejoicing at the thought of being with Christ face to face.

I thought only of my son back in the states.

I thought of each painful way I could die at the hands of this madman.

I thought of the people and responsibilities back home.

I was distracted by so much.

I didn't think of being embraced by God who loves me beyond words.

At that moment, my faith had been weighed and measured, and I had come up empty.

So here's the point. The moral of the story, if you will:

> Simple statements have the power
> to change the way we think forever.

But there's more than a moral; there's meaning:

Henry: It's been seven years and two months since my first trip to Haiti and just under two since I was here last. I usually don't know this date, but I looked at it on my passport as I flew into Port-au-Prince this morning. After reading Dani's story on the plane, the eternally happy Leonard, picked us up with his usual smile in the bright green happy bus.

I am currently upstairs at Gertrude's guesthouse, our traditional Haitian home away from home. I am listening to the children whom she has taken in play, sing, and laugh with my team. It is different to write here, but it seems so right for this story. I am using paper and pen as the sweat beads on my brow and drips to smudge these words.

It is different to read the story here.

It is different to recall my friend's words,

> "At that moment my faith had been weighed and measured
> and I had come up empty."

From stage Dani speaks those words with conviction and the

authority that only comes after the hard work of repentance.

Repentance is another one of those words that carries a lot of baggage. In high school, I remember being shouted at by the dirty, grey-haired man wearing the sandwich board that read, "Repent or Perish" on one side, and "Turn or Burn" on the other. He stood on the corner of Rudisill and Calhoun, where my brother and I would ride our bikes in the summer. Some called him a street preacher, but I only heard distorted yelling through his megaphone.

That placard and the disconnected man with his holier-than-thou attitude was intrinsically linked to my baggage with the word "repent." His words planted seeds of fear and anger that drove down roots of resentment. Rather ironically, over time those roots blossomed into the same attitude of anger that he had initially displayed - until I learned what "repent" meant in Greek.

Metanoia is the word. Actually it is a compound word. "Noia" is "to think" or "to think different." The word "meta" means "after". So repentance or "Meta-noia" means to think different after.

It would have been easy for Dani to ignore what happened that day. She could have taken that first breath, and then another and just moved past that experience, but she didn't.

She repented.

She stopped and thought differently after that experience.

Once I learned what repent means, I repented of my anger too.

Dani: The conversation around repentance is a hard one. For most that have hung around a Church for long, the phrase calls on our need to repent of a sin and then to receive forgiveness. Far too often, for those outside of the Christian culture and even for those inside of it, the word evokes much of the hatred that Henry spoke of. Rarely do people use the word "repent" for describing their response to a situation that changes them; instead it remains a habitual association with sin.

While it carries weight in how we live our lives, repentance still exists outside of sin. I had to struggle through my assumptions and false understanding of "repent" to fully grasp how it can be used in shaping my character and living my life. When I keep repentance linked only to how I move forward from sin, I miss a great opportunity in how it can move me forward toward maturity as a human being.

'Repent' and 'forgive' are often used interchangeably, so understanding the difference behind these words will add richness and depth to their meanings. On the cross, Jesus took all sin upon Himself and conquered death. He claims for us, "It is finished."[1] If all sin is forgiven, then why do we have the call to repentance? Why must I confess my sin if I am already forgiven and live as a free person? After all, God says, "as far as the east is from the west, so far has he removed our transgressions from us."[2] The span that separates the East from the West is infinite and immeasurable. This illustration is so beautiful for the simple fact that God has cast our sin as far away from us as possible, never to be remembered. Forgiveness is mine and has been all along.

Repentance, then, is for me, and not for God. I need to acknowledge to myself that I have fallen short and done wrong. Only when I repent – when I think differently after – do I have the opportunity to change the way I live and the way I think.

Henry: Before we move on from it, I want to press into this strong link between repentance, forgiveness, and sin a bit more. Each of these words has roots in the Greek language. We have begun to talk about *metanoia*, the word that is translated as "repent" even though a more literal translation would be, to "think different after." Likewise, we discovered the true meaning of *hamartia*, the word that is translated as "sin." Rihanna helps me understand these two words together. Maybe God is saying something through her when she sings,"

Don't tell me that you're sorry 'cause you're not,
Baby, when I know you're only sorry you got caught.[3]

If I wrote hymns or worship songs I would steal these lyrics.

How often have I claimed to repent of sin when really I am not thinking differently about it at all? I will claim to be sorry, but in my heart I know I'm not. Many of us have gotten good at feigning remorse; but we know we'll repeat the same broken behavior because we never think differently about it. Sure, we can get better at hiding it, and masking it, and not getting caught. We will, however, destroy T.R.U.ST with others, and God, and even ourselves unless we truly repent.

I didn't think differently about "repent" until I started hanging out with friends who looked at repentance without linking it to sin or forgiveness. Through them, I realized that I had repented in the huddle of the football games of my childhood, long before I even knew what repent meant.

My mother called me, 'a late bloomer'. Matt Bock and Brian Greiner were the first to hit puberty when we were in 6th grade. The fact that they were 7 or 8 inches taller than me didn't mean a thing in the classroom. Our friendship was not affected by the extra 40 pounds of muscle they had that I didn't. But when they were both on the line against me on the grade school playground, these differences did matter.

They mattered a lot.

I don't remember whose idea it was, but when the two biggest guys in the class ended up on the same team and we were getting whipped, my team got creative. It was third down and we knew they would blitz. So we came up with this play: I would snap the ball and then the quarterback would touch it quickly, bouncing it back to me. Matt and Brian would blow past me as I pulled the ball back through my legs and would run like crazy. In the huddle it seemed brilliant.

I remember grunting "break!"

I remember snapping the ball.

I do not remember how I ended up on my back so quickly or how long I had been lying there.

I do remember it hurt really bad. But my face was OK and I still had all my teeth.

So I went back to the huddle and repented with my team. There was the thought before the play. Now it was after and did I ever think differently after. In fact my whole team repented of that play.

I've got a lot of friends in AA who tell me, "Insanity is defined as doing the same thing but expecting a different result." That is why we repent, isn't it. If we are getting the results we desire, there is no need to repent. We really only repent because what we were doing didn't work as well as we'd like it to.

That is why my whole team repented of that play.

That is why we should repent of sin.

How many Christian's look at porn, skip repentance and simply feign sorrow when they get caught? In doing so, we miss the point, don't we? What does it look like to really think differently about what is going on?[4]

To realize these are people with hearts and dreams and not just images projected on screens. These are sons and daughter who you are participating in violating. Then there are all the hidden ways these subtle glances affect your relationships. The way you've trained your eyes to look at the people you meet and the T.R.U.S.T. that is broken with your partner. When we enter into repentance, rather than reciting mere words, these are some of the thoughts that we must think.

If you have hung around Church, chances are you have heard that sin breaks God's heart. Repentance calls us to ask why. As we

actually think differently after *hamartia* happens, sin might start to break our hearts too.

I want to think differently about *hamartia*.

I want to think differently about God.

I am desperate to have my thoughts align with a heavenly story, rather than one filled with bull. I don't want to minimize *metanoia hamartia*. Yet perhaps Christian's need to learn to repent, even when it has nothing to do with sin, so that we can truly repent from sin.

Dani: Yet how do we deal with repentance? How are we able to process moments and let them change our lives, rather than just sweep them under the rug and continue with the status quo?

Haiti and other countries with endemic abject poverty face extensive problems and have few vague solutions. Poverty and corruption has never been easy. Neither has been processing death, or divorce, or lying, cheating, murder, or cancer; nothing difficult is ever easy to process. There are two keys however, to aid with repentance: artistic space and our pairs of T.R.U.S.T.

Henry: Have you ever looked at a professional painting up close? I mean press-your-nose-against-the-canvas close? Of course not. First, you would be kicked out of the gallery. Second, everybody knows that you can't see the masterpiece without stepping back to take it all in. "Artistic space" is the distance that is needed between you and the painting to see what is really going on. In my experience, the concept of repentance, as thinking differently after, needs this kind of artistic space, even if it is rather brief.[5] Repentance isn't thinking differently in the midst of, it's stepping back and thinking different after.

I could not think differently in the midst of getting knocked down playing football. I couldn't really even think in that moment. Dani could not collect her thoughts enough to breathe in the moment she locked eyes with the machete-waving madman. Nobody could. But we can think different after.

We are told that when God put the sun, moon, and stars in the sky,[6] they were put there to mark days, years, and sacred moments. I don't want to read something into the Bible that is not there, but in my life these have worked well to create the kind of artistic space needed for repentance.

Each and every day I am greeted by people who ask, "How are you?" Since I live in an American culture, I respond, "Fine." Why do I do this? Part of it is simply social kindness, but this works because in the midst of the moment, I'm on autopilot. I don't really think about the question at all. Each day though, I allow the sun, the moon and the stars to mark my life. I carve out a little bit of artistic space each morning before I move into my day and each evening when the day is done. In this space, among other things, I really answer the question of my culture's greeting. In these moments where I step far enough away from my day to actually see it, repentance happens.

This artistic space, and the subsequent repentance that over time, changes the way we think in the moment. I think this is what the Apostle Paul hints at when he talks about being "transformed by the renewing of your mind."[7]

Dani: We see how naturally it comes for Leonard to think a certain way. His mind has been transformed and conditioned to live in a place of peace, mostly because of the rhythms he creates. There is artistic space built into his daily and weekly life. Many Haitians don't work until they crash; they work steady, they take breaks, and they pace themselves.

Sacred moments are also necessary artistic spaces. One of the great losses in American culture is the absence of Sabbath. The Sabbath is a key structure built into the fabric of what our spirit needs. God intentionally asks us to observe Sabbath because it benefits us. The

Sabbath requires that you slow down, pay attention, enjoy, relax, and let the experiences of your life settle into your spirit. You have a healthy amount of time to feel the weight of your life.

Henry: In 2004 my family started our journey toward celebrating a weekly Sabbath, marking a sacred moment. The Sabbath is a day when we strive to produce nothing. A full 24 hours where we find our identity not in the things we create, but in the One who created us. It took my family about six years to get to the point that it was a regular rhythm; we needed to learn to think differently about a lot of things. Paradoxically, it was this kind of space that allowed us to think differently about what we did the week before and what we planned to do in the next week. This day allowed for minor course corrections rather than huge overhauls.

Then there is the marking of the years. Each year, around June 14, Tricia and I celebrate the anniversary of our wedding. The very first time we marked the year, she looked at me over dinner and asked, "What is your best memory from our marriage?" I didn't know it at the time, but what she was really saying was "Let's repent. Let's look at that favorite memory from this year and try to make more like them." This is a transformative experience where we celebrate, and in the celebration we give room for repentance.

Dani: It is healthy to learn how to live with different levels of artistic space in our everyday lives. As a mission trip leader, I find it a critical tool in helping people process what they have seen in a place that feels very different from what they are used to. Right after breakfast there is group devotions; a time set aside to prepare for the day. After we return from our work day, there is required solitude time. This allows all the sights and sounds and experiences to settle into each person. We then close our day with reflections and more devotions. All of these create necessary artistic space.

Henry: On my most recent trip to Haiti, I used the schedule artistic space to reflect on previous trips. I thought about my very first trip, when riding home from work one day I had no hope and saw no evidence of a heavenly story.

We drove past yet another lot filled with garbage where three emaciated goats stood atop an eight foot heap. A stream oozed from beneath the rubbish and gravity did her work pulling the ooze down the hill. As we drove on, there was a car pulled over to the side of the road and a man looking at the engine. He was standing in the midst of the this stream as he attempted to repair his broken radiator. The neon green coolant mixed with the ooze and caused a faster flow. A bit further down stood a man relieving himself into this same stream.

What broke my heart and stole my hope, is what I saw next. Several hundred meters downstream, out of sight from its source, sat an infant. Her mother lovingly bathed her in the stream, just as my wife bathed our daughters in the kitchen sink back home. For the first time on the trip, my stomach churned because of something other than the stench.

The problems were too big and too systemic. I am a "fix it" guy, but as we drove I couldn't think of a single solution. That night, seven years ago, I had no hope. Perhaps that is why I didn't return for five years. Although my faith was weighed and measured, I had no conviction because I never repented. I thought, but I did not think differently after that experience; because I had not taken the need artistic space.

I was fortunate that as I repented, I had a pair. Phil had been on the trip with me two years ago, so like me he wasn't just processing each day as it came; but he also had years of artistic space.

Dani: Pairs of T.R.U.S.T and learning to repent are difficult to live in the reality of life. God gives us the ability to learn from our experiences so that we can grow to live abundantly. One of the hardest parts in repentance is learning to trust another person with your thoughts. When we think differently after and let another

person know our thoughts and emotions, there is always a chance they will think of us differently and turn away.

When Paul and I had to cope with our first miscarriage, we had very different responses. It was difficult to be honest with one another. Paul was ready to be a parent, where as I was left with more questions and was unsure. I wondered, could I trust him with my heart and my fear of raising a child when he wanted one so badly? He wanted what I was afraid of. Our repentance in this situation caused different reactions, and in order for our marriage to stay strong, it required that we be honest with one another.

Sitting with a picnic lunch on a beautiful summer day, Paul and I cried with each other confessing all the truths that we had been hiding. We took a chance to continue building our T.R.U.S.T relationship by admitting what we felt. We understood the different struggle that our partner had and could support them, uplift them, and respect their process. Repentance happens in relationships with T.R.U.S.T.

Henry: Sometimes repentance is just known by two, like it was surrounding Dani's miscarriage. Other times it plays out within the context of a larger group. I saw repentance work through my team in Haiti first hand.

Phil told me that our team was down. They were feeling despair and hopelessness. Their faith was being weighed, measured, and they were coming up empty. Of the nine other people on this trip, only four had been in country before. However, they had experienced nothing like Port au Prince, with its four million people living in very limited quarters, competing for even more limited resources. Two were in the rural mountainous part of the country a few years back and two were a newly-wed couple that had stopped at the beach of Haiti during their honeymoon cruise.

As we drove by the fenced-off, fractured remnant of the Cathedral, it got to them and cracked their hearts. The earthquake was four years prior and a simple chain link fence was the only improvement we observed. Tarps were tied to the top of the fence and staked to the ground, providing makeshift homes for many. Why was nothing being done? Why was there such abject poverty in the shadow of holy ground? These thoughts stir up despair.

But my team hadn't seen the picture two years ago.

They had no 'after' from which to think differently.

They couldn't repent - at least not yet.

As Phil and I talked, we reflected on two years ago. No one had yet fenced off the ruins. Standing within them, I met a man whose legs had been amputated because they'd been crushed by the crashing steeple during the earthquake. He was living in the dilapidated cathedral with a three-legged dog he had adopted. As he made a joke that it must be his dog and pointed at the missing legs, he told us that the crime was getting bad. All the marble had been stripped from the building. Another man pounded at the concrete with a rock, attempting to steal the rebar in the center. The man without his legs looked at the man with the rock as he explained just how bad it had gotten and whispered that these men got violent if you looked at them while they stole.

To most on our trip, it was a travesty that the only difference was a simple fence. To Phil and I, it was a baby step forward. In being a pair to the rest of our team we helped create the space needed to repent.

Dani: It always amazes me what a little bit of time can do for my understanding. Leonard was my pair of T.R.U.S.T that day on the bus. I changed the way I thought because I saw a better way, a heavenly meaning in the way my friend lived his life. Truly embracing the identity given to him by God alone, Leonard showed me what it looked like to live as a child of God.

I repented and changed the way I saw myself. It was the same way

Kelly saw herself even when she was at risk of losing it all. She held onto the only thing that was strong enough to ground her. When life was attacking her, challenging who she was with lies of who she wasn't, she held onto her covenant identity and trusted God to be enough.

One of the reasons I love reading the gospel of John is because he so often refers to himself as "the disciple that Jesus loved."[8] John lived out this identity in everything he did, much like Leonard. Looking back on this story I was struck with how hard it is to repent and truly move forward and think differently.

After my jet ski accident, I thought differently about my identity. I confessed how so much of who I thought I was got wrapped up in how I looked. In the days and weeks after that event, God worked on my heart and revealed where my true self was broken.

I repented.

However, fast forward to me on the bus where my identity was threatened in another way, and again I came up empty.

It is a strong challenge to fully accept your true identity and allow the false self to fall away. My story has revealed to me how often I must continue to repent from my false selves and live into my true covenant identity.

It is the only way to fully embrace my life.

CHAPTER 8:

Shiny Red Blessings

~by Henry

As a child I never had to mow the lawn in the summer, because I had allergy-induced asthma. I was not allergic to snow however, so I couldn't get out of shoveling. Every winter I would put on my snow pants and my jacket, my boots and my gloves, and that hat with a fuzzy ball on top. I was then sent out to shovel.

I outgrew the snow pants and jacket, and grandma knit me a bigger hat that still the fuzzy ball on top; but I never outgrew my allergy to grass, so I never had to mow it. Yet, I've continued to shovel on every blustery morning after a snowfall. When it snows in Indiana, you don't just shovel the driveway once. The snow falls so often, you have to shovel several times even in one day.

This went on for thirty years, and then I decided to leave the world of shovelers.

One wintry morning, it started to flurry just a bit and the weatherman was predicting a good solid, couple inches of snow. In anticipation, I stopped by the hardware store on my way home. My decision had already been made, so I did my best negotiating and drove home to unload my new shiny red machine.

After I screwed on the handle and filled her up with gas, I went to bed like it was Christmas Eve. I was ecstatic as to what the morning would hold. There was really no surprise when I woke up before my alarm. When I looked out the window, I saw a clean white blanket of fresh snow had covered our neighborhood. I checked my phone to see the school delay confirm that it was a good snow. Everyone was allowed to sleep an extra two hours. But that morning, I couldn't sleep.

I had a rite of passage to get to.

I went to bed a shoveling boy and awoke a snow blowing man. No snow pants or hat with a fuzzy ball would be needed this morning. Just my boots, a coat and gloves would serve me well for the brief time I expected to be outside. As I laced up my boots, I glanced out the window at my neighbor. His driveway is as long as mine,

but even steeper and much wider. He can almost fit three cars in the garage. Then his driveway V's out from there, expanding even wider toward the street. I have even seen them park another car on either side of the driveway. The night before the snowfall, they had actually done just that.

My neighbor was about two thirds of the way done shoveling behind the car parked on the left. Knowing from my past shoveling experiences, it was going to be a long morning for him.

The garage opened and the wind stirred the snow into a frosty mist. In my mind's eye it felt like a scene from the silver screen. I looked at my phone to check the time. It was 6:54 am. I started the snow blower with one clean pull and began to blow snow. I was amazed at how fast this was. I wondered why I had not purchased this a year ago. I was thankful and whispered to God, "Thank you for this blessing." My cheeks hadn't even turned rosy red and my driveway was already half done.

In this brief time, the word "blessing" floated around in my mind several times. I thought about when Abram was called in Genesis 12. Before you think I'm more holy than I am, I knew I would be preaching on this text in a few days. I also knew I had to finish the bulletin notes later that day. Even a two-hour delay wouldn't give me more time before Sunday's sermon.

The words God spoke to Abram were, "I will bless you to be a blessing." I wish I could claim my motives were pure, but I knew I'd be preaching and I was looking for a good story for my sermon. When a story isn't coming you've got two choices: make one up or attempt to make one happen. That day, I decided to take a stab at the later.

As I finished my second to last pass, I noticed my neighbor was still shoveling behind that first car. I decided that since God had blessed me with this new snow blower that I must have been blessed to be a blessing. I was going to help my neighbor out. By

the midpoint of my final pass, the story had played out in my head and my sermon was writing itself. What would happen next became a grandiose vision of not just a sermon story, but a testimony from him.

I imagined it playing out like this: I would offer to help him with his driveway and he would be amazed and befuddled by my generosity. As we finished his driveway he would ask, "Why would you do such a thing?" I would exclaim, "God has blessed me to be a blessing, freely I have received, freely I will give!" (That would preach, right?) To this he would reply, "Tell me more about this God who blesses." I would preach Christ crucified as the ultimate free gift and he would fall to his knees. The warmth of his body would miraculously melt enough snow to baptize him right there in the driveway. Then his wife would look out the window and see what was happening and invite me in. She would give us hot chocolate and the children would come down from upstairs in footed pajamas to see mom and dad studying the Bible together.

I may have ditched the little hat with the fuzzy ball on the top, but my wild boyhood imagination still ran rampant. So with this image in my mind, I walked across the cul-de-sac and said, "I got a new snow blower, can I give you a hand?"

He had finally started shoveling out the car on the right side of the drive when he gave me an odd look.

"Nah, I got it," he said.

"Seriously," I exclaimed looking down at my phone and noticing it was only 7:04. "My kids are on a two hour delay. I have tons of time and would love to help."

"I'm good," he said as he went back to his shoveling.

I walked back across the cul-de-sac, pulling my new snow blower behind. As I trodded through the snow, I noticed tire tracks into my next-door neighbor's garage. I remembered that he was

working third shift and had gotten home in the pre-dawn hours, after the snow had fallen. He would be asleep until noon and then have to wake up and shovel.

By this time I was ready to be a blessing to a neighbor no matter who.

It didn't matter if they wanted it or not.

I wasn't even looking for a sermon illustration at this point.

Honestly, I was a bit peeved.

So I went over to his driveway and as he slept I cleared it with my new snow blower.

As I walked back home, excited to be a blessing, I noticed my other neighbor still hadn't finished the area behind his second car. Even when he finished that, he still had the majority of his drive to shovel.

So here's the point. The moral of the story if you will:

> Often we miss out on a huge blessing because we reject it, other times we are blessed even though we don't realize it.

But there's more than a moral; there's meaning:

Henry: When we found out Tricia was pregnant with our first child, I was amazed with how many pregnant women I saw. Then a few years ago I bought my first new car. It was red, and sure enough everywhere I looked, from the highways to the alleys, there were new red cars. Psychologists and neurologists have told me that this has to do with my reticular activator. I don't really know what that means, but I know that it is the same way with stories. I hope that you are starting to have the same experience and are seeing stories everywhere.

The key is not just to notice stories, but to let them become more than a story and I am convinced that this only happens when we discuss them with others. That morning, I thought the point of the story was what you read above; that there are so many times I missed out on something because I rejected it. I've since discovered

the point is even bigger.

Several years ago Tricia had hurt her back and we racked up a ton of medical bills. We blew through our savings and were praying that God would provide. Then one Sunday after church one of the women came up to Trish and said, "I just got my tax refund and usually donate it to something. I know it has been a tough year for y'all and as I've been praying about what to do with the money; you keep coming to my mind. Would you accept this gift?"

When Tricia told me about this, my reaction was hesitance.

My reaction intrigued me, because I had been praying that God would provide for us. My friend had been praying about what to do with extra money. I was in the midst of a mini-miracle, and my reaction was to hesitate!? I now know that ego and pride and the myth of self-reliance were having their way with me. The point, though, is that I almost missed out on a huge blessing.

Dani: When we strip away the funny parts of the story and Henry's fuzzy hat with a ball on top, what we are left with is how the rejection of a blessing results from pride; something many people struggle with. Pride in its simplest form is thinking that you are higher than you are, that your life, opinions, needs and stories are better than another's. Pride, was the downfall of Adam and Eve in the Garden of Eden. It feeds an egocentric lifestyle that you are the center of the universe and everyone around you is there to meet your needs.

When we dig further, what we see is how pride keeps us from blessings while control influences our choices in whom to bless.

Henry: Each of my girls when they were very young loved to grab my hands and jump. Before the very first jump they would say, "Watch how high I can jump, Daddy!" and then they would leap into the air. Sometimes they would come close to hitting their heads on the ceiling. Other times they would flip upside down as they jumped and hang in the air pretending to walk on the ceiling. They

giggled with glee as I sang and their walking turned to dancing. Since they have gotten bigger they can't jump, holding my hands any longer; but we have built an arsenal of amazing memories.

The truth is we both know they were not jumping on their own. There is not a three or four year old in the world who has a four foot vertical leap. Even if there were, we know they couldn't defy gravity and walk on the ceiling. My girls could jump high because I was helping them.

Could you imagine if in the midst of dancing on the ceiling they said, "Daddy I can do it by myself," and I obliged. The old saying "Pride goeth before the fall," would be enacted right before my eyes. In truth, no one can do it by themselves.

The reason why a posture of humility is much better than a posture of pride, is that because it has more truth. Humility is neither thinking too highly of yourself, nor too lowly of yourself; rather, humility is not thinking of yourself. Neither of my daughters were thinking of themselves as they danced on the ceiling; instead they were enjoying the moment.

My friend Mychal is really good at a lot of things; yet, I've never seen him get prideful about them. I've noticed he has a habit of saying, "They let me." On our church softball team, he was the slugger. In fact I think he's the only guy to hit the ball out of the park during our tournament. Playing church softball would not even make his resume; Yet, I have heard him say more than once, "They let me play on the church softball team." He doesn't just say this about softball, but about his job and about the basketball team he was the captain of in college. Mychal does not just say this, he means it. His identity is not found in what he does, if it were, what would he be when he was in a hitting slump? Because he knows who he is, he can live in true humility and consider even playing church softball a privilege.

Pride is simply when I make it about me and what I do, and forget

all the others that have made it possible for me to be doing it. Pride forgets the pair. Pride blurs our identity and often fools us into thinking that we are what we do, making us concerned that we are indeed the one doing it. It would have been a lot easier to accept the gift of money, if I realized that even having my job was because, "they let me be their Pastor."

Like it was for my daughter, the fruit of such humility is laughter and dancing. Let's face it; being held up by the strength of another and dancing on a ceiling is much more fun that worrying about how high I can jump on my own.

The sad truth is, that control or the illusion of control, is often the fruit of such pride.

Dani: We saw what pride does to our ability to receive blessings, but what of control? We love to decide who receives our blessing, and if they are worthy. We cast judgment on people and their lifestyles. We decide who has a right to our time and our money. This is often played out even in the small acts of kindness we show to the people who live around us. I learned a huge lesson in judgment and controlling my time and gifts in the midst of a Minnesota snowy winter.

Living in Minnesota, shoveling turns into a daily chore for five months straight. What I love about Henry's shoveling story is how it echoes my own. This is often the case when we talk about our stories and share them together.

One blistering, cold day, my daughter and I had just come home from dropping her brothers off at school. For the third day in a row we were getting ready to shovel. That morning, I remembered a woman who lives three houses down from us. Her husband was out of town for two weeks which left only her working full time, the grandma, and her 2-year-old daughter. I thought it would be kind if I could help out and do this one chore for them so she wouldn't have to do it after work and bear the cold, and risk slipping on the

ice. Easy enough right? Shovel your neighbor's walk, and in 15 minutes I would be done.

My confession is that I don't often think about helping my neighbors by shoveling their walks, or doing other chores. The sad but true reality is that I go about my business and do my own thing. I get my work done and then move on to the next project on my list that revolves around me or my family. That previous Saturday however, my middle son came out to help me shovel and I thought this was a good activity to teach him how we can help people in all sorts of ways, even on our own block. It saddens me that I often will only think of helping others when I know it will help me teach my children about compassion. I have a long way to go in understanding a full change of heart.

So, that Saturday, we shoveled for them.

A few days later, I was out there again shoveling more fresh snow. I thought to myself, *no one is here to see me or learn from me. Why aren't I shoveling my neighbor's walk again?* I will go and serve my neighbor because it is the right thing to do. I can bless them again because I have the time and am able to do this. However, in order to get to their home, I needed to pass my immediate neighbors, who are Hmong. I have lived next door to these neighbors for more than 10 years and never once have I shoveled their walk. They don't speak English, but we have lived peacefully next door to one another, watching our kids play together for years. The grandma has helped me weed my garden and we have shared plates of food with each other every time a baby is born in either home.

Would I really walk past my Hmong neighbor's snowy sidewalk and not help out? There are 15 people who live in that house. They have many capable hands that could shovel; but just because they can shovel, does not mean I couldn't show kindness to them. I decided to keep shoveling from my walk down to my neighbor's.

The house after that is the new house with the neighbor that I

struggle with the most. They have a little boy who is hard for me to love. His relationship with my children has been tough and has included bullying. This young boy has taught my children every naughty word in the book; all before they were five. His aggression is sometimes hard for me deal with. However, *is his family not worthy of kindness? Would a kind act not show them compassion and a little bit of joy?* Convicted, I kept shoveling.

After the new house is the home that has been abandoned since a tornado ripped through our area almost two years earlier. After the tornado, it has sat neglected with all doors and windows boarded up. It now sits with a "For Sale" sign on the lawn. Truthfully, all the neighbors loved when this family left. Whereas the little boy in the new house is hard for me to love, this whole family was *really* hard to love. There were all sorts of shady things that happened in that house. Cops were regularly there, and a few years back these neighbors received a lot of attention for shooting and killing their dog in the basement.

The abandoned home was the last house before the woman I was trying to help. I decided to shovel that walk as well. I don't know if anyone was going to come and do the shoveling. I doubted it. Yet, I thought of all the people who would walk the sidewalk getting to the bus or to work, and I thought about the mailman. I shoveled it for them.

Finally, I shoveled the walk I'd set out to.

As I went about my chore, I thought about all these things.

I thought about the family who was capable and had lots of people to shovel.

I thought about the family who kind of scares me.

I thought about the empty home with no family, that holds so many past mistakes.

I thought about the family in need.

I realized I was placing judgments on who was worth my time and kindness and who was not. If I am going to be upfront about it, I need to admit that I so often size up and gauge who is worth my time and energy.

For me, asking those questions revealed how dark my heart is. It revealed to me the depth of my selfishness. *Are only the people with the greatest needs the ones worthy of my time?*

After the shoveling was done, I noticed that all I did was reveal the ice underneath the snow. I was filled with despair as I realized I did more harm than good.[3] I went into our home and got our bag of salt, thinking to myself, *"Now I have to go and buy more salt because I am going to use it all up, and I wasn't planning on spending money on this."* It would be terrible for me to shovel, only to reveal ice beneath, and do nothing about it; then to have someone slip, seriously injuring themselves. In that moment I realized how God was pushing at the darkness in me piece by piece.

"Just give a little bit more. Give a part of yourself till you can feel the pain of letting go of a part of you, your stuff, your money, your time for someone else. I want you to feel giving. I don't want you to just be a convenient servant, because that is really no servant at all."

I continued until I had salted everyone's walk. I was annoyed, but I knew it was the right thing to do. I knew God was teaching me in this moment and shaping my heart to look a little more like His, and I am thankful for that. I did not say anything about what I did to my neighbors or to my children. This was just about serving and loving the people around me.

I am not sure my neighbors would know we are Christians by the way we live. They see us go to church, and we talk about kindness and love in our home. They know we are believers, but that is only because they have asked. I am ashamed by how little I have done to serve the people right here on my street. That statement right there is why God is shaping my heart. He is reaching in for the darkness

to replace it with light to shape the community in which I live.

I should mention that it snowed for the next four days. Every day, there was a new layer on the ground and I experienced God reached deeper inside me. I was being challenged with questions about selfishness, giving and serving. Questions like:

Where is the line for loving your neighbor?

Is loving someone once and blessing them for a moment enough when the moment happened at your convenience?

How do we decide who is worthy of our blessing and when they stop being worthy?

How far do we interrupt our lives to give part of our time and heart to someone else?

Henry: These are such good questions to wrestle through, and I don't use the word wrestle lightly. I'm realizing that so many "Bible words" have taken on a meaning very different than the original recipient would have understood. One of these words is "bless" or any of its variants "blessing" or "blessed." What does it really mean that Abram, and by extension you or I, are "blessed to be a blessing?"

Usually I think of a blessing as something good: a new snow blower, having someone do something for me, or a financial gift. While I'm not discounting this, I think it is far too shallow. Does this kind of blessing mean the same thing as when Jesus delivers the beatitudes in the sermon on the mount? Is there a way that "Blessed are those who mourn" can vibe with "blessed to be a blessing?"

The more I dig into this word the more I'm convinced of its incarnation essence. When Jesus says "blessed," I believe He is saying "God/I am with you."[4] Look at Matthew 5:3-11 and see if understanding "blessed" as "I/God am with you" doesn't make more sense than pretending "blessed" is always about having something material.

3 "Blessed are the poor in spirit, for theirs is the kingdom of heaven.	3God is with the poor in spirit, for theirs is the kingdom of heaven.
4 Blessed are those who mourn, for they will be comforted.	4 God is with those who mourn, for they will be comforted.
5 Blessed are the meek, for they will inherit the earth.	5 God is with the meek, for they will inherit the earth.
6 Blessed are those who hunger and thirst for righteousness, for they will be filled.	6 God is with those who hunger and thirst for righteousness, for they will be filled.
7 Blessed are the merciful, for they will be shown mercy.	7 God is with the merciful, for they will be shown mercy.
8 Blessed are the pure in heart, for they will see God.	8 God is with the pure in heart, for they will see God.
9 Blessed are the peacemakers, for they will be called children of God.	9 God is with the peacemakers, for they will be called children of God.
10 Blessed are those who are persecuted because of righteousness, for theirs is the kingdom of heaven.	10 God is with those who are persecuted because of righteousness, for theirs is the kingdom of heaven.
11Blessed are you when people insult you, persecute you and falsely say all kinds of evil against you because of me. (NIV)	11 God is with you when people insult you, persecute you and falsely say all kinds of evil against you because of me.

Please know, I am not saying that understanding financial abundance as blessing should be discounted, rather it should be framed in the light of Emmanuel, God with us. I believe God was with Abram so he could truly be with others. Our identity is found in our wrestling with these deep questions and in our wrestling with God.

I am using this term very literally. Abraham's grandson, Jacob, received his identity and the subsequent identity of God's covenant people by wrestling with God.[5] That is what Israel means, "To wrestle with God".

To fight by wrestling is very different that to fight by boxing. Boxing is done at a distance whereas wrestling is done up close. In wrestling the one tries to shape the other. When locked up in a wrestling match one actually hears the heartbeat of the other. I believe this is what happens when we wrestle with the things of God. When you wrestle with questions like the ones Dani just spelled out, we hear the heartbeat of God and are shaped by it. In wrestling we are blessed; that is, God is with us.

CHAPTER 9:

Mac and Cheese

~byDani

My family and I live in a neighborhood called North Minneapolis. One block down from our home, is a beautiful park that my kids and I walk to almost every spring and summer day. On our way to the park, we pass our neighbor Lyvester's home. As we walk, we stop, we pet his dog, and we make small talk about the neighborhood, work, and the weather. You know neighborly things. Then we say our goodbyes and head over to play on the playground.

I remember that it was Monday June 8, because Paul and I were celebrating our anniversary. We didn't have a sitter, so we decided to cook a wonderful meal at home and enjoy it after the kids went to bed. I fed the kids an easy meal while I made Paul's favorite foods. I had steak marinating, potatoes boiling, pumpkin pie chilling and green beans steaming.

While the kids were playing, I heard a knock on our door. When I opened it, there was Lyvester, standing at the bottom of our stoop. He was wringing his hands together and looked nervously at the ground. That he had come to our home told me something was wrong. He never came to our home. All of our social interaction was in his yard on our way to the park.

I greeted him and tried to welcome him inside. He kindly rejected my offer and proceeded to anxiously tell me about some trouble his sister was in. She needed to get away for a few days, so she dropped off her two young girls at his home while she went and got help. He gave details about how he would get his food stamps on Wednesday, but as it was Monday, he didn't have anything to feed his nieces. He came to my home wondering if he could borrow five dollars to go and get a couple cans of beans or cereal, until he could take them to get real food the next day at the homeless shelter.

He was ashamed.

He was embarrassed.

His body language was screaming that he did not want to be standing on my stoop asking such a hard question and admitting

that he had no other option except me or the homeless shelter.

I was struck by the overwhelming feeling of abundance in that moment. My in-laws had just been to our home and filled our freezer and pantry with food. We walked the aisles and picked out not just food we needed, but fun food that we wanted. Yet, just a few doors down from me sat a family with, literally, nothing in their cupboards. Here we were grilling steaks and veggies, dessert was waiting and wine was chilling in the fridge. Everything felt wrong about this moment. It was wrong that I would have so much when my neighbor had so little.

After a few moments, I finally convinced Lyvester to come into our entry way while I went to get him some food. I confessed that I didn't feel right sending him away with just a few dollars when we had more than enough to give. I called the kids and they came into the kitchen to help.

I gave my young kids a simple explanation that Lyvester was having his nieces stay over at his house and he needed some food to feed them. I grabbed a brown grocery bag and shared with them that we were going to help. I got down on my knees and asked them, "What is your favorite thing to eat?"

They immediately replied, "Macaroni and Cheese!"

I asked them if they thought these other girls might like Mac and Cheese and I was rewarded with a resounding "Yes!"

We put our last box in the bag. I then asked what we needed to make Mac and Cheese.

They thought for a brief moment and then exclaimed, "Milk and Butter!"

Clearly we ate our share of this favorite meal that they would so easily know in detail the ingredients that went into it. Into the refrigerator I went and grabbed a new gallon of milk and a stick of butter. At this point my children were bored, and they went to go

play. I finished up by putting some cans of green beans and corn in there along with some other goodies and healthy food.

When the grocery bag was full, I went out and handed it to Lyvester. His eyes got big and then filled with sorrow at accepting such a gift. He hesitated in reaching out and grabbing it. I looked at him and reminded him that we had just been abundantly blessed, so we had lots to share. While taking the bag, he immediately told me he would pay me back. He could bring some of his food stamps over to me on Wednesday when he received them. By taking my gift, he absolutely felt the need to pay for it. I looked him in the eye one last time. I took his hands, full of the groceries and said in my most convincing voice, "We have been given so much; it is my joy to share it with you and your nieces. Please do not try to pay me back for this. Many people have helped us along the way; it is just such a pleasure to be able to do this for someone else. Please just enjoy this time with the girls."

He accepted, but as he left he continued to tell me that he was going to find some way to repay us. He walked back to his home, just a few doors down from mine, and all I could do was stare and be overwhelmed with feelings that I couldn't sort through. I couldn't believe I didn't know my own neighbor was struggling so much. How did I not know?

So here's the point. The moral of the story if you will:

> Sometimes you can't choose who or when you're going to serve,
> the need just shows up and then you can't ignore it.

But there's more than a moral...

Henry: I used to think money was what was needed to make a difference. People need more money, or at least more access to it. More money would solve so many problems. Then I learned that most people who win the lotto, blow through the cash in a short amount of time and end up in the same, if not worse, financial situation then when they started. It had been a few years since

I discovered this so, I checked to see if that was still the case. A simple Google search revealed the headline "How One Lottery Winner Blew Through $10 Million in Less Than 10 Years.[1]"

Naively, I thought more money would solve the problem.

Then I thought if we could only teach people to manage money, then problems would be solved. I wrestled with these thoughts the night after my mission team almost started a riot in City Soleil. The city is more of a shanty town built atop the old garbage dump outside of Port au Prince. Shortly after President Aristide was exiled, the poorest of the poor fled to the dump knowing they could survive there on what was once considered garbage.

We had filled the back three rows of Leonard's happy green bus with hundreds of pounds of rice, packaged in gallon zip lock bags. We had distributed these bags at a church earlier that morning, where they gratefully stood in neat lines. Parishioners and Pastor assured us that each bag would feed a family for days. City Soleil, with 400,000 packed into 8 square miles had a different feel.

As we began to distribute the rice, hundreds of hungry people descended upon us in moments. The disordered excitement escalated to chaos quickly. One person grabbed three bags while another had none. Two men, each grabbing an the same plastic bag pulled it apart and the rice rained to the ground causing an instant dogpile of children. Desperation turned to rage when we announced there was no more.

When we are in Haiti, we always travel with light security, generally a plain clothed Haitian police officer with a side arm. That day was no different and he was the one who announced we were out of rice. He told us to "get back in the bus," as the crowd surrounded him yelling and began to push. Several of the men from our team watched intently, but Leonard encouraged us to get in the bus. When everyone except our security, who was still in the midst of the mob, was on the bus Leonard said, "No Problem," and began

rolling forward.

The Bible tells a story[2] of a mob in Nazareth that was ready to kill Jesus and He simply walked through them, unscathed. As I watched our security guard emerge from the riotous crowd and step onto our now moving bus, I had a picture of Jesus' story to pull upon when I read Luke 4.

Still, as I lay in bed that night the chaos of the day fading, I thought of valuable resources like cash and rice. I thought about how we could teach people to manage such resources better. I layed there with judgement in my heart. Brene Brown said "if you judge yourself when you ask for help - you always judge others when you offer help." I was living this. As my thoughts drifted from them to me. I wondered, could I manage my own resources better? Who was going to teach me such things.[3]

I'm a solution guy, and as I searched for solutions, I thought about resources and the scarcity of them. Was the problem a lack of food? I remembered a sermon, or maybe it was a Vegan activist at the local co-op say, "There is enough food in the world that no one has to go to bed hungry. The issue is simply distribution." Remembering those words, I had three thoughts. First, why do people say simply when it is not simple at all? Second, why can't I remember if it was a preacher or someone from the Co-op who said it? Third, what resource is most scarce?

I placed fresh mango on a piece of toast I had slathered with peanut butter moments before. This act felt odd as I pondered scarcity. Then I heard a voice from above that gave me clarity. It was Kim calling down, telling the team that devotions started in 5 minutes.

It became clear to me that money wasn't the most limited resource. I can always get more. There are tons of ways to get it: work for it, steal it, borrow it or print it. Sure, some ways of getting more money are easier and some are harder. Some of these ways are ethical and others aren't, but I can always get more.

It was the same way with food. My brother grows it. My wife shops for it. Lyvester asked for it and the residents of City Soile almost started a riot for it. There are ways to get more of this resource too.

But the resource Kim was announcing from the rooftop is truly the only limited resource.

Time.

Each person has the same 24 hours each day. Nobody gets more and nobody has less. How we manage this time however, makes all the difference in the world.

As I crammed my toast into my mouth and headed upstairs, I thought about how I was spending my time. How much of it I was using on stupid stuff like flipping through channels not even watching a show. How many weeks had I wasted being angry or holding a grudge? I thought about moments that seemed to last forever and weeks that flew by too fast. I reflected on how I was investing it and where I was getting a good return on my investment. I don't know why, but at that moment I remembered a quote from Mother Teresa "If you judge people, you have no time to love them."

Dani: Managing our time, the awareness of judgment in our hearts and how to help humanity is complex and instinctively intertwined. After we have judged who is worth our time, it is only then we set out to help humans in need. Time is our one limited resource. Who will make the cut in earning our precious and coveted resource? Years ago I heard a speaker challenge her audience to step out in faith and respond to God's call of serving and loving other people. She told us, "The need is the call, when God is revealing a need to you, then He is calling you to do something about it."

This stuck with me and I haven't been able to live my life the same way since. When I live under the belief that "The need is the call," then my eyes and ears are always open to see where God is calling

me to respond. It becomes far too easy to reserve my compassion for a time set aside for serving. There are moments when I go about my busy life and I don't notice the old woman crossing the street who needs help, or the mother with the screaming baby who just wants to try on shoes at the store, the kid who is lost at the park, or the veteran with a sign standing on the street corner. I want these needs to call to the compassion that lives in me.

I believe it is common for everyone at some point to wonder what their calling or purpose is in life. As a believer, many people want to know what God is calling them to do. Some men and women never make a move without first getting a sign from God. They wait searching and holding on until they "feel called" to do one thing or another.

The truth behind, "The need is the call" is how it breaks down these philosophies, challenging us to step outside of our theology and ideology and look at the real human needs right in front of us. We see the needs that cross our paths on a daily basis. These needs are mental, physical, spiritual, and emotional. When we wait on our expectation of how God is going to call us to move, it is a direct injustice to the great need of humanity. God reveals his heart to us through the everyday faces, pain and hurt of those around us. He challenges us to see Him in the brokenness.

Henry: "A place for everything and everything in its place." I love that concept. It helped me when I was a camp counselor years ago. It gave me a metaphor for this book. The reality is I really do want to be a tidy and organized person; but life happens. Every couple of months or so I clean my office both at home and at work and try to put everything where it goes. I have these little dividers for the drawers in my desk so I can make a vain attempt to compartmentalize even my junk drawer. I claim it is so I can be more productive and get things done in the right way; but the truth is I use all that organizing as a distraction. I cannot begin to tell you how many times I have avoided writing this book by sorting

files and organizing junk drawers. The truth is, I don't write better in an organized office than I do in a cluttered one.

For a lot of years, I tried to live my faith the same way I approached this book. I went to college and seminary trying to get all of the clutter cleared so I could respond to the call. The reality was, when one fuzzy thing was cleared up and put in its space, thirteen more would appear. If we wait until our lives are clutter free to start answering the call, we will never answer it at all.

What I like about living in a "the need is the call" kind of way is that it happens in the midst of the clutter. It happens in the messiness that is considered life. If I try to compartmentalize my life to "ministry time," and "work time," and "family time," and "devotional time," I never really get any of them done. In fact I'll spend most of my time just trying to compartmentalize.

Don't get me wrong, this "need is the call" lifestyle is all on a spectrum. It is not either organized and compartmentalized or organic and integrated. It is both. As a child I loved watching the tightrope walker at the circus. Over time I realized that the big pole he carried reached both to the left and to the right. In order to stay in the middle, the tightrope walker needs to reach out in both directions.[4] When I have my organized devotional time and my daughter walks into the room, I can not say, "Family breakfast isn't for five more minutes, you're not on the schedule yet."

Rather, I sit her on lap and finish my devotion with there. I need to carve out time for the important things like devotions, and family, play, work, and ministry. More often than not however, when I plan to go "minister" to someone, it just won't happen. Yet, when I'm playing with my kids in the backyard, we will both see the need and be able to respond to the call. The reality of the phrase is that it is a lifestyle, not a program.

Dani: I think we can all admit to saying "I have nothing to eat in this house" while our pantry sits full.[5] Sure it may be stocked with

food we don't want to eat or food we have to cook, but the fact of the matter is, food is still in our house. Lyvester came to my home asking for a few dollars so that he could feed his nieces. In order to consider a can of beans a meal, your pantry really must be empty. How desperate it must feel like to look in your kitchen and truly have nothing.

Supporting the local food shelf is a really easy way to give to those in need. Many schools, business and organizations are coming up with creative ways to include a canned food drive in their ticket sales or entrance fees to events. Even the post office usually has a day where they will collect a bag of food off your door step to donate to the local food shelf. Everyone wants to do their part. I must confess though, when I participate in donation drives like these, often times it is my excuse to empty out my cupboard. The first items I give as a donation are usually the items I am tired of eating. Those items that were part of a diet I am not on anymore, or food that is now gathering dust because I bought it with good intention to use someday. That is what a program looks like, but a lifestyle is more. A program is a start; but a start is different than a story.

Mother Theresa once said, "Don't just give, give until it hurts. Give until you have given a piece of yourself away.[6]"

Jesus said, "When you give to the least of these, you give to me.[7]"

I was ashamed at my behavior before, at the way I treated the nameless and faceless people that use the food shelf. I gave them my cast offs, the things I no longer wanted or needed. I didn't think, "What would they like to eat," but rather, "What can I get rid of". That is all too common with programs. We don't engage with people who need the program, so the program becomes something that starts to serve my need.

When reflecting on his documentary *Shadow's of Virtue*, Chad Amour says, "Often the programs we create to serve the needs

of those around us often become the idol that displaces those in need.[8]"

It becomes about my need to serve someone.

My need to clean out my house.

My need to feel like I am doing something good for humanity.

The tragedy in this, is that it isn't the program's fault, it is our own selfishness we need to battle.

I was not seeing the person in need, but rather they were the object that spoke of my own selfish desires. I wanted to feel like I had helped someone. Helping someone else makes me feel better about myself. When giving becomes about me and serving my own need, the person I am serving is then an object to reach my goal. This is simply objectification.

But now, the person who needs me, the face of the man at the food shelf was Lyvester, my neighbor, and I couldn't ignore him. I was so convicted in that moment when he came to my door needing my help.

Henry: It really has to do with roots and fruit. There is an apocryphal tale of the influential father speaking to the Ivy League Dean at his son's freshman orientation. The father explained the great potential of his son, how he had excelled in elementary school to the point of skipping seventh grade. He boasted of his son's grade point average, honors credentials, and extra-curricular activities. Then he asked the Dean, can't my son be fast tracked and leap beyond all the introductory and prerequisite classes? "He just has such great potential," the Father explained.

The Dean listened as he tamped his pipe and looking the father dead in the eye said, "Clearly, your son is a bright boy and certainly could be fast tracked at many universities. It doesn't take a full season to produce a cabbage; but here we grow oaks." With that, the dean lit his pipe and walked away.

The difference between a cabbage and an oak has more to do with what happens under the surface, than it does with what happens above it.

Understand, I want to squelch all rumors right now and go on the record saying I'm not against programs. Getting five bucks off of a cover charge, in exchange for a couple of cans of food, has a bunch of great effects.

It puts a meal in the belly of a person who might not have otherwise had it. This is a good thing.

It keeps issues of poverty and hunger in central focus. This is another good thing.

It also serves as an entry point for many who want to get involved. Yet, another good thing.

However, if we are honest, these things only go so deep and while cabbages have their place, let's not pretend they have deep roots. Academics, entrepreneur, and people much smarter than I am have come up with better solutions than the current "program model" many use. However, in the midst of all the programs, I think the real problem is quite simple.

What our heart longs for, the thing that will change the world, is more than a story. Programs are, by definition, less than a story. Have you ever heard anybody sitting around after the concert telling the story of handing the bouncer a can of cream of mushroom soup and saving a couple bucks?

I haven't.

First, it's just not a story you'd bring to the table. When I was working on homework with my daughter, her grade school textbook said a story needs: plot, character, conflict, theme, and setting.[9] Programs lack in at least some of the basic elements of a story. A program is a start, but it's not a story.

Even more problematic than programs lacking the basic things

needed for a good story, is that there is no pair. The bouncer collecting the cover charge isn't a pair. The band "requiring the donation," which is a funny concept in itself, isn't a pair. In most cases these people never even have a chance to be a pair because we don't even really know them, let alone T.R.U.S.T. them.

When we use programs, which keep others at an anonymous arm length, as a substitute for this kind of messy interaction with the bull of life, we rob the potential of story. With no pair and insulated bull, how can we even hope for the fruit of a good story? After all, fruit is what we are really looking for. But, if we walk around looking for and picking fruit, it will quickly run out. If we desire fruit for years to come, we must plant seeds of story and wait as the roots of those oaks grow deep underground and unseen. A neighbor is always full of potential pairs. When like Lyvester, they stand on a stoop owning their bull, the fruit of *more than a story* is ripe for the picking.

Dani: In the previous chapters, we established our need for people to help reveal deep truth and meaning in the stories of our lives. These relationships, or pairs of T.R.U.S.T., are set apart because of the accountability and honesty they hold. They make us honest because we can't hide from the people closest to us. They are too close to our story. Inasmuch, they hold us accountable to the truth of the stories we tell. However, as human beings, we need to realize that each one of us is connected to each other. Beyond pairs of T.R.U.S.T. it is important to see how we do not exist outside of other people. Humanity is intricately connected. When one group suffers, we all suffer. Our American culture has somehow convinced us that our individuality and personal value is set apart; that we ourselves are the most important. We each are the center of our own universe. We look inward to find our identity, but identity is always given.

The real truth and greatest discovery of ourselves however is when we lose ourselves to the service and love of other people.[10] I believe

this is what Christ is guiding us towards. It is what I experienced with Lyvester. When my focus became the other person and his needs became more important than my own, I experienced freedom from selfishness. We find fulfillment in helping others. We discover our strengths and weaknesses and what we are capable of. We find there is depth in our soul that we would have never discovered unless we were encouraged to dig that deep for someone else. When we stop looking at ourselves, we find true joy and acceptance of who we are in the whole of a community.

Jesus' brother James wrote a letter to the Jewish Christian believers. In it he writes,

> Religion that God our Father accepts as pure and faultless is this, to look after orphans and widows in their distress and to keep oneself from being polluted by the world.[11]

This verse points to the complexity of living for self or living for others.

When I first understood this text it was sitting in a Bible Study where all the participants discussed the struggle around the last portion, "keeping oneself from being polluted by the world." It struck me how the focus of this group was just on the second half of the verse. Not one person looked at God's call for us to engage in helping the poor and living for others. The conversation was solely directed toward how to keep pollution out of our hearts, which is self focus. They had flipped the plot, confusing the cause and the effect.

In order to let the full impact and understanding of the truth that waits for us in scripture, we need to read it in its full context. It is dishonest to pull out the bits and pieces that we like or that support our own personal theology. Scripture is a complete work, with all the pieces working together. The problem lies not only with pulling pieces of scripture out of context, but most importantly putting the end before the beginning. The words of God become polluted when we don't read it as it is written. When we look at the

second part of this verse, we are exclusively "self focused". When we read it in full, the "others focus" becomes very clear.

CHAPTER 10:

What a Twister Stirs Up

~by Dani

It was around two o'clock on a Sunday afternoon and our children were taking their naps. Paul and I were snuggled on the couch finishing a movie we had fallen asleep to the night before. It had been storming all weekend, with no sign of letting up. The sudden darkness caught our attention though as the sky went from rainy grey to almost midnight black. The lights flickered and Paul and I watched the wind pick up. We heard a faint siren go off that seemed to be at least one city away and we looked at each other.

"That doesn't mean us, does it?"

He just shrugged. In the eleven years we lived in our home, we had never experienced a storm that forced us to hide out in the basement.

The wind took on a vengeance, and we knew then that we were already too late. We grabbed our kids from their sleep and dashed for the stairs. We shouted upstairs to our housemate Chad, who looked outside and saw the same thing that we did. He was already on his way down. We were mere feet from the basement when our ears popped. It was the first time I had ever experienced that feeling. At that moment, in my heart, I was scared. I knew something bad was coming and we weren't ready.

I made it to the basement with my daughter Lu while all the boys made it to the stairs as the power flickered out for good. My two young sons, Noah and Caleb were only part way down the stairs. They couldn't make it the whole way though because they couldn't see anything in the darkness. They started screaming and trying to run back up the stairs where they thought it was safer. Paul and Chad were yelling to convince them to get downstairs as they heard the windows blowing out behind them. During all the screaming, my daughter squeezed me with all her might. She buried her head in my neck and held on for dear life. She was filled with tension and I could feel her tremble with worry.

Somehow the men got the boys downstairs, and together we crammed in among the suitcases, winter clothes, and games in the closet under the stairs. The only light to break the complete darkness of the room was the soft glow of Chad's iPhone.

The only thing the light revealed to me was the sight of sheer terror on the faces of my children.

What could I expect after they had been ripped from their beds while sleeping and shoved into a scary dark closet in the basement? The deafening freight train noise and glass breaking only made matters worse.

I looked at Paul and Chad with worry. I wondered what we were going to do next, and how we were going to help the kids handle whatever we found upstairs when this was all over.

After being in the basement for a handful of moments, it seemed the worst was over. We could hear the wind soften, the rain lessen, and there were no more sounds of anything breaking.

Paul and Chad went upstairs to assess the damage and make a plan. I stayed in the basement and sat with my kids, arms around them all, listening to their worried voices asking if we were going to die.

"What's happened mama?"

"Are we going to be OK?"

"I'm so scared!"

I held them tight, and reassured them that we were OK, we were together, and God was watching over us. I sang their favorite songs to calm them down and pass the time.

We got the "all clear" to come up. When we walked through our kitchen, I got a good look at what had happened. The first thing I noticed was that our beautiful climbing tree that had once sat against our garage had been uprooted, tossed across the yard, and was now pressed up against the kitchen window. As we kept going, I had to stand still and take in what had become of our house.

There was glass everywhere. It looked like birthday confetti.

Branches and tree limbs littered our furniture and floor.

It was raining inside our home through all the broken windows.

Everything was wet.

I thought, *"How do we help the kids process this? They're so young. How do we deal with this, talk about this, approach this? Is there anything that will give them peace in the midst of this crisis?"*

I had no idea.

Paul and Chad emptied the shattered window glass out of the kids shoes and brought them to us while we waited in kitchen. With the amount of glass everywhere, walking anywhere was unsafe. Once we knew their feet were protected, we were able to walk outside.

We looked around our yard and down our street, and it was surreal.

I saw fifty year old trees lying on the ground, glass shattered and covered the sidewalks, and shingles were wedged in the grass sticking straight up. A tree limb was plunged in our car, furniture was tossed about all over our yard, and fences were bent, broken and ripped to pieces. Many of our neighbor's garages were just blown away. There were swing sets in the streets and power lines were scattered like silly string.

We started making calls to everyone we knew in the area.

"Are you alright?

Is anyone hurt?

How is your home?

How far did this thing go?"

What felt strange in this situation was that before really comprehending if this was all real, all I saw was a movie set. Movie scenes look just like this. Stage Designers spend days putting together a disaster that looked like my neighborhood, except this time, it wasn't a set. It was real.

Then I realized it wasn't just real life.

This was my life.

I could only stand there and take it in.

I saw parts of homes missing. There were also couches, windows, garbage bins, grills, rakes, potted plants all just lying outside in the middle of the street. I stood there in shock, realizing this was now my story.

My neighbor's garage landed on my newly planted garden. The week before I had spent three long days building a sturdy wooden fence around it; now there was a garage on top of it.

I looked across the street, and so much of my neighbor's living room and garage had been ripped apart that I could see through into their backyard. Everyone then started coming out of their homes, just like in the movies. They were frazzled and confused. I saw neighbors I never knew I had. Neighbors were going door to door making sure everyone was accounted for and alive. Once we were sure everyone was alright, there became this moment of…

Now what?

What do we do now?

Where do we even begin?

Paul began by making lists of what we needed.

Chad and I began by making sure the kids didn't step on or touch anything dangerous. The boys were little and wanted to explore everywhere. Lu had just turned one and wanted to put everything she touched into her mouth. We were at a loss of what to do in that moment, the needs were so vast.

So here's the point. The moral of the story if you will:

Tragedy illuminates and magnifies who people truly are.

But there's more than a moral...

Henry: When I was young, Will Smith was a rapper who went by the name of "The Fresh Prince." As the door to the TV show bearing his stage name swung open, fame and money were right behind it. Rap was getting big and money was streaming into artists hands. Explicit language, violence, drug use and other abuses seemed to accompany this genre. The newsreels showed rappers being lead out of court in their orange jumpsuits. Headline after headline talked about how money had changed these men, somehow corrupting them. I was just starting my first summer job and must admit I was a naively afraid of what the $85 a week would do to me.

Then there was Will Smith. He was being interviewed because of a large donation he made to start a charity for at risk kids. The interviewer was perplexed by the paradox between the simple generosity of this rapper and the criminal exploits and opulence of so many others. Smith's blunt response to her question shocked her and rocked my world.

"Money does not change people," he said.

The Fresh Prince went on to explain, "Money just magnifies what was there all along. Those guys have always acted like that: greedy, criminal, abusive. All the money did was made these traits bigger and more visible."

He then claimed that he wasn't being more generous. He was simply doing what his mom had taught him as a child.

"If we didn't share as kids, my mother would whoop us," he laughed.

He was just sharing as he always had. I think Will Smith was right on. Money is simply a magnifier and an illuminator.

Tragedy is the same.

It doesn't matter if it is a Tornado in Minneapolis, an Earthquake in Haiti, or the Super Storm in New York. I mention these tragedies specifically because I've had friends at the epicenter of each. My friends have all attested that the tragedy they experienced illuminated and magnified. The stories they tell only vary in detail; the cut and thrust remain the same.

My friend Tim leads a church on Staten Island. We were talking a couple of weeks after the storm had hit in October of 2012 and relief efforts were well underway. Tim was seeing tragedy as a great illuminator and magnifier of character first hand. I was hundreds of miles away reading the Mr. Rogers quote that flooded Facebook for a few weeks after the storm:

> When I was a boy and I would see scary things in the news, my mother would say to me, 'Look for the helpers. You will always find people who are helping.'

I saw the evening news spinning that same story. Years ago I had bought into the rapper myth that money corrupted people. Now, like so many, I was buying into a myth that tragedy made people helpers.

I'm pretty sure my friend Tim has never been compared to Will Smith, but what he said rocked me out of this myth the same way Will had so many years before.

Tim said, "Tragedy like this just brings out what people are. The leaders lead. The manipulators manipulate. The whiners whine. The storm just brought everything to the surface."

Dani: If tragedy brings what lives deep down inside of us out in the open; then most of life is lived within the confines of social kindness and politeness without ever getting real. It is socially expected to say to someone in trouble, "Please let me know if there is anything you need. Call me if I can be of assistance." I believe people when they say that to me. I truly think they mean it, to

some degree. However, it often feels like the social equivalent of, "I'm fine," in response to the question, "How are you?" Though a well intended question and answer, it stays socially safe. Saying those little words doesn't commit me to your pain. It requires no investment on my part. It doesn't insist that any of the compassion I have rises to meet your need.

I have spent years leading trips to serve in Haiti; but I've always been on the giving end.

Now, here I was, standing on the other side in the midst of an emotional war zone and the aftermath of a physical tornado that had wrecked my community. I didn't know what to do with offers like, "Please call me if you need anything."

I knew people meant it, but honestly, I had no idea what I needed. I think I needed everything and I didn't even really know what that meant.

I also was not sure if they really meant what they said.

If I needed a sitter for eight hours, could I call them?

What if I needed a meal dropped off because we were so busy making insurance calls and cleaning that I didn't have time to cook?

Could I really ask someone to do that for me?

Even more than not really knowing what I needed, it felt wrong to ask, especially for the big inconvenient stuff that was necessary. We needed help boarding up our home, cutting up the huge tree in our back yard, a generator, a babysitter for days, and food. Being on the giving end, I know how wonderful it feels to do something for someone who needs help. However, it is really difficult to ask for it, even knowing that people genuinely want to love you in that way. I don't like asking people to spend their time and money on me. I don't want to be an imposition on them and their life. It feels wrong to say, "I know you have a life and are busy, but can you drop everything and come over to help me pick glass out of my yard for a few hours?"

It is hard to ask for help.

Then, without asking, my friend Inga, showed up at my house and told me she was going to take the kids for the night. She didn't ask or offer, she just showed up. She told me to pack their pajamas and she would take them so Paul and I could make a plan and figure out what to do. I felt so relieved by this.

Then our friend Jeromy called and asked, "How many windows are broken? How many trees are down? Can you get into your garage?"

He asked all the dad questions that I couldn't wrap my head around. He showed up 30 minutes later chainsawing his way down our street to get past all the fallen trees to help board and tarp our home.

Paul's boss Scott called asking a long list of questions about supplies we needed. Before heading our way to help out, he picked up everything on the list so we didn't have to worry about it. He even included extra supplies for our neighbors.

That night my friend Tabitha called me, offering to take the kids the next day so that Paul and I could clean away all the broken glass. She was happy to watch them for more than 9 hours hoping Paul and I could put a dent in the cleaning that was needed.

Our Pastor organized rides for my kids to get to swim lessons, people to bring groceries, and took a collection to help us pay for repairs.

Paul and I felt overwhelmed by the people who pushed past social kindness and showed up, in our crisis and helped us cope.

Henry: This concept of social kindness and pushing past it is not unique to turbulent times. I have a friend from Australia who was amazed that his American phrasebook wasn't exaggerating when it warned that "How are you?" is a greeting and not a true question. The book then listed the proper responses to this greeting as "fine" or "OK," followed by "and you?" The first time we met, I fell into the American script and he responded "fine and you."

When I said, "OK," he actually started to laugh out loud.

Through his chuckle he replied "You really say that, Mate?"

This was back in the days when even though I wasn't flying I could walk right up to the gate and meet him. We hadn't even made it to baggage claim and we had each fallen into our cultures script of social kindness.

As an American, I've been trained to ask questions that look like I care, even when I really don't. As an Aussie, he was socialized to call me "mate," Australian for friend, even though we had just met at the gate and we hadn't built that kind of relational capital yet. This kind of social kindness is all around us, so much so, that we often don't even recognize it. Jesus talked about social kindness with His disciples.

Jesus tell His disciples "When you enter a house give it your greeting[1]" but, He doesn't tell them what to say. It seems that every age and every culture has a socially kind greeting and they knew what it was. If Jesus was talking to a Texan today they would know to say, "Howdy Partner" and my Aussie friend would assume, "G'Day Mate." Likewise, Jesus' first century Jewish audience didn't need Him to explain that they should say, "Shalom." The word that means "Peace."

Social kindness is commonplace in greetings. Yet, even back then Jesus and the disciples understood that there are some people who lived in this social kindness. Some people who said peace, didn't mean it. Then there are some who push beyond the social kindness; or as Jesus says, "who receive you with peace."

Today, I think Jesus would have still instructed us to use the common social greeting; but then unpacked it in our cultural context. He might have said something like,

> If they really answer and tell you how they are doing, and then really want to know when they ask how you are; invest

your time there. If they say "Fine, and you?" move on without shame.[2]

Social Kindness isn't bad. In fact, it's a lot better than social meanness. A "Hi, how are you?" even when we don't really want to know, is still better than ignoring people as you pass by.[3] Social kindness just is what it is. Jesus doesn't tell His disciples to plow through it, or attempt to tear it down. Rather He tells them to invest in the people who are going beyond social kindness.[4]

Dani: Social kindness serves a purpose. It often keeps people at a safe distance from one another. But, never pressing beyond it is the opposite of building T.R.U.S.T. relationships. T.R.U.S.T. relationships are too personal to stay at a safe distance. T.R.U.S.T. relationships require compassion. They insist that you get in the mess with the people you love. Tragedy and money illuminate how deep people are willing to go with you. When storms and hardship hit; pairs of T.R.U.S.T quickly come to the surface.

The friends mentioned: Inga, Jeromy, Scott, Tabitha and Pastor; stand out in my mind as the ones who shape this story for me because they didn't settle for social kindness. They came in, invaded our space and helped pull us out.

I believe we have each experienced an emotional, or mental, or even physical hell, where we can't see the way out. No one can get out of tragedy alone. You don't know which step to take first because each step feels like the wrong one. You feel like the darkness is so overwhelming that you can't even see the pieces, let alone begin to put them together.

When you get into someone's pain with them, you will at the very least offer them comfort. Often times you can be there to help guide them out.

For one of the first times in my life I saw how the body of Christ was designed to be, and it was beautiful. The actual tornado almost becomes an afterthought to the way people came in and took care

of us. We were rocked to our core as friends came from all over to be with us. They found jobs and ways to help, each person filling a different role. The parts of the body were working together. For the next few weeks I saw 1 Corinthians 12:12-27 lived out.

> Just as a body, though one, has many parts, but all its many parts form one body, so it is with Christ. For we were all baptized by one Spirit so as to form one body—whether Jews or Gentiles, slave or free—and we were all given the one Spirit to drink. Even so the body is not made up of one part but of many. Now if the foot should say, "Because I am not a hand, I do not belong to the body," it would not for that reason stop being part of the body. And if the ear should say, "Because I am not an eye, I do not belong to the body," it would not for that reason stop being part of the body. If the whole body were an eye, where would the sense of hearing be? If the whole body were an ear, where would the sense of smell be? But in fact God has placed the parts in the body, every one of them, just as he wanted them to be. If they were all one part, where would the body be? But God has put the body together, giving greater honor to the parts that lacked it, so that there should be no division in the body, but that its parts should have equal concern for each other. If one part suffers, every part offers with it; if one part is honored, every part rejoices with it. Now you are the body of Christ, and each one of you is a part of it.

Henry: Looking at T.R.U.S.T. relationships and pushing beyond social kindness started the gears in my head turning. When Dani said she saw the parts of the body working together, it threw a monkey wrench into those gears. *What part of the body was I? What did this tragedy illuminate about me and who I really was? Was I really a T.R.U.S.T. pair with Dani and Paul?*

Over the decade, between meeting a dainty Dani who used a fork and knife to eat mozzarella sticks, to now sharing the stage as speaking partners, I thought we had built T.R.U.S.T. I had been in their wedding, we had traveled the country together speaking and we even had a joint family vacation planned for later that summer. But when I found out the tornado had hit them, it illuminated all kinds of bull.

I should explain that while I keep my pulse on pop culture, I am chronically behind on news stories. I catch up on the weeks big stories when on Sunday morning people say, "Pastor, can you believe..." When my befuddled look gives me away, they bring me up to speed. Since, the tornado hit on a Sunday afternoon, I was lucky that I found out about it by Tuesday or Wednesday. When Inga was picking up kids and Jeromy was chainsawing trees, I was ignorant that tragedy had even struck my good friends, Paul and Dani.

By the time I found out what had happened, I was still 592 miles away. I claim to be part of the1 Corinthians body Dani said she saw in action, but where was I? I started to wonder if I lacked compassion, since I hadn't pick up a chainsaw, or child.

Then I remembered this little spot in the middle of my back that I just can't scratch. It's not even an inch above my farthest reaching finger if I stretch behind my back, chicken wing style. If I reach the other way, over my shoulder, it's then just a bit too low.

I get frustrated trying to itch that spot, but then I realized that sometimes, that is the part of the body I am. That spot I can't scratch is right on top of my spinal chord. I'd never claim it wasn't an important part of my body, but still I can't reach it, no matter how hard I try. This reality was illuminated by the tragedy my friends were going through so many miles away.

My hand, not being able to serve the role it seemed like it should, doesn't mean it has no role. My hand can still open my office door so I can use the frame to scratch that spot, bear style. Likewise, even though I was far away, I could still send encouraging emails, be a sounding board, and pray.

That's why tragedy is such a great illuminator and magnifier. It

doesn't just hit one person or one issue.

Dani: Our tragedy in that storm illuminated the deep compassion in the people around us. It brought out what we knew was there, but I was still speechless when the giving didn't stop. Even after a couple weeks, the phone calls and the support and the meals didn't stop. I love watching the body of Christ work this way. It is the closest I can get to seeing the heart of God played out here on earth.

Looking back on those days and weeks after the tornado are some of the moments I've felt most spiritually alive. God used the people around us to meet us in our pain and pour love in our life. Having that experience allowed my T.R.U.S.T. relationships to build and strengthen with these friends. Not only did it change the way I trusted people, but something systematically changed in my relationship with God.

There was a level of trust I hadn't breached with Him before that experience. Through the tornado, God magnified a deep level of commitment to my family that I wasn't fully aware of until then. I watched as He took care of every little detail, not leaving us alone to shoulder this burden. He showed up in every way possible through all the people in our life.

I also was seeing how this experience was shaping my character.

My attitude and perspectives were changing.

My understanding and empathy was growing stronger.

My commitment to compassion was becoming more alive.

It is healthy to step back and see what tragedy illuminates in others, but what about what it brings to the surface in us? What does an extreme situation bring out in me? The tornado revealed a very deep sense of judgment in me that I wasn't expecting. Something I am not proud of and am working on repenting from.

Henry: Anything that illuminates; illuminates without prejudice. You don't get to choose what you see. There is a storage space, under the stairs in my basement. In the front, it's got a few shelves and is the perfect size for storing cases of T-shirts or books I will take on the road with me. Since it's under the stairs the back part is where I stick stuff that I really should throw away. Somehow, I convince myself I will use it again someday. There is not light in this closet, which is fine because the light from the room lets me see the front and I rarely need to see the back.

The other day I was looking for a box and it wasn't in any of the normal box places in my house. After looking for a while I took out the front two layers of nicely labeled boxes in the storage under the stairs. Knowing I could now see to the back, I went to get a flashlight. When I turned that light on, it didn't just illuminate the boxes I wanted to see; it lit up all the junk I didn't want to see too. Junk I should have just thrown away, stuff I should have put together and used by now, plus there were dust bunnies and a few cobwebs that I had to deal with.

When we say "tragedy illuminates and magnifies," we have to own and unpack that this isn't just what we are looking for. In the previous chapter, you read "if you judge yourself when you ask for help - you always judge others when you offer help." This kind of self judgment was illuminated in me because of my distance and magnified in Dani as she stood on the other side of giving and receiving.

Dani: I became aware of this judgment when I was sitting on my stoop with my daughter in my lap after the tornado. I was there watching not only my children, but the other neighborhood kids play on the weather saturated couch that was now in our front yard. They were dodging shingles which were sticking up out of the ground and crunching on the glass that was everywhere. They were picking up broken tree limbs and battling with them as swords. I was the mom sitting on her stoop allowing all the dangerous play to happen. I couldn't begin cleaning; because every time I started, my children would jump in too help. The surest way to keep them safe

was to ignore it, because they learned how to play around it.

We had no electricity.

We had no windows.

We had no car to go anywhere.

This dangerous playground on our front lawn was the only thing we had. It was the only place to go.

As my kids played, I saw them coming. The church group wearing their matching mission T-shirts and coming down my street carrying water bottles, business cards and compassion. As they got closer, I saw one of the gals assessing my yard and situation. I saw her gauge the danger in what I was allowing my children to do, and then I saw her look at me.

It was the look of judgment.

Let's be honest, I would have judged me too if I saw a woman doing nothing to help her situation, sitting on the steps while her children play with rusty nails, nasty couches and glass.

Judgment is such a strange thing isn't it? We do it all the time, often without even thinking. On one side of the coin we do need healthy judgment to make sure we stay safe in scary situations, or with dangerous people. Judging and assessing risk is important and good. There is however always a dark side to judgment, the one that is hypocritical, and self-righteous. The type of judgment that make us appear better than we are and always cast others in a negative light.

Henry: Dani and I were sitting and having coffee with our friend Dave. He makes his living doing hip-hop, so he has a flow even when it is just with friends catching up. He just can't help it. We sat and discussed perspective with stories and how so often we don't have the full picture. He shared a catchphrase that stuck with me. He said that we all needed to view others with an MRI, Most Respectful Interpretation.

How it works is this: There are always some observable verifiable facts. For example one day I was standing just outside the revolving door at a Children's hospital next to a sign that said "No Smoking within 8 ft. of entryway." Right next to the sign there was a woman smoking. In one hand she held a cigarette and in the other she carried her oxygen tank, which was still pumping through the tube in her nose.

Everything listed here is a fact, but chances are you made an interpretation.

I know I did, and mine was anything but an MRI. My interpretation was that she was disrespectful, caring neither for her life nor the health of the sick children walking in and out of the door. I thought to myself "can't you read," and must have given her that kind of look.

Then a security guard approached her, said "Ma'am" and pointed to the sign.

She looked at it. Dropped her cigarette and collapsed into his arms. I heard through her weeping "He didn't make it. My boy is dead."

Any interpretation is simply that, and in this case mine was very wrong. There was no disrespect in this woman, simply shell shock. She wasn't a woman who didn't care about the sick children but a mother mourning the loss of her own. If my interpretation could be so wrong in that instance, when else could it be wrong? Knowing there is that much room for error, what if I chose to actively put the best spin on every situation, striving to give everyone an MRI?

Dani: The stories we live give us something to understand about ourselves and humanity. The more we have conversations about these stories, the more knowledge and empathy we gain. Once we are able to empathize with others, we can let go of the "us and them" mentality. We then live in a perspective of shared humanity, acknowledging what we have in common, and not what separates

us. An MRI helps shape your perspective, and perspective is a necessary tool to eliminate judgment out of your spirit.

Shared humanity is the realization that the pain, or joy, or suffering I experience is not only limited to me, but something that most other people have felt or experienced. I am not alone with my broken heart. I am not the only person who has ever felt lonely, unseen, insecure, or prideful. These are common human emotions. When we embrace our shared humanity, we have less time to judge, and more ability to show compassion. Our perspective puts us all on the same side, instead of standing opposed to one another, casting judgment that tears at someone's character.

Perspective grabbed hold of me and changed me. As I sat on my own stoop watching the "helpers" come, all my preconceived ideas and judgments and solutions fell into place. I understood now what it felt like to be so overwhelmed and completely numb because the disaster felt so big I didn't know where to start. I recognized in that moment that we never have the whole picture. We don't ever really know what is going on in someone's life. We catch glimpses and base our whole understanding of that person and their life in that one moment. We need to respect people enough to give them the benefit of the doubt. I want to give the people I meet that live and behave differently than me a healthier MRI.

CHAPTER 11:

I Wanted To Get You Flowers, So...

~by Dani

My husband and I met for the first time when I was 19. It was a brief introduction before we went separate ways. We assumed we would never see one another again. Seven months later, we ended up working at a youth conference together at a hotel in Chicago. He was there to do Comedy Improv while I was there selling merchandise for the two bands playing.

Looking back, we were never really friends; there was chemistry right from the beginning. We were drawn to each other, aware when the other one entered or left a room. I noticed when he laughed and he paid attention to who I was talking to.

After that weekend, we went our separate ways once again. Paul was living in Minneapolis while I still lived in Detroit with my parents. He began to write me letters, a timeless token of affection.

Two weeks after receiving my first handful of letters, we spoke on the phone for nearly seven hours, neither one of us wanting to hang up as we learned so much about each other. I knew in my heart even at that point, I couldn't walk away from a man like Paul. I was young and it scared me to know that I had already found the man I wanted to spend my life with.

We married nearly three years and countless love letters later.

We stayed in Minneapolis and purchased our first home with a friend of ours. It is an old bungalow just on the outside of the city. We lived in its small apartment type flat on the second story for many years, where the only door in our place was to the bathroom. Living in such a small space with virtually no privacy, Paul and I learned the importance of communication.

Three years later we had a six month old baby boy and were on our way to a BBQ to celebrate the birthday of a dear friend. Even with all the regular ups and downs of a relationship, I still only had eyes for Paul and he repeatedly told me he would never find anyone he loved as much as he loved me. People around us would roll their eyes. Who am I kidding, writing this I want to roll my eyes.

Driving to the party, we stopped at a store to pick up a handful of items for supper. I gave Paul a five item list; he kissed my cheek with a sparkle in his eye and promised to be right back. I sat in the car with a sleeping baby, listening to music, I let my mind drift. That day, as it is often known to do, my mind drifted toward the amazing man I was blessed to call my husband. I was thankful that somehow we had been able to hold onto this beautiful relationship for all these years. I was overwhelmed with how much he always showed me the depth of his love. He showed me through words of affirmation, small presents, doing chores around the house, taking me out, and other sweet gestures[1]

Somehow in those few moments sitting in the car, I had moved from appreciating the way Paul loves me, to convincing myself that when he walked past the buckets of flowers on sale at the checkout counter, he would be so moved by his love for me that he just could not resist buying me a dozen roses as a token of his undying affection.

Imagine my surprise when I saw him emerge from the store, a small grocery bag in hand and nothing else, headed towards our car.

There were no flowers.

There was no token of affection.

And so I did what I've always done when I am confused and frustrated but don't have the words to articulate why. I gave him the cold shoulder. As he got back in the car, he gave me a kiss on the cheek and I gave him an attitude.

My shift in mood was obvious. No longer was I the happy wife waiting for my love's return. I instead sat as a jaded woman who felt misunderstood and under-appreciated.

I watched as confusion washed over Paul's face. In his effort for good communication, Paul asked, "What's wrong?"

Apparently in my effort for avoidance, I replied, "Nothing". Even as

the word crossed my lips, I knew it was lie.

Listening to that word, he knew it was a lie.

Anyone who has ever spoken or listened to this response knows it's a lie. Yet, why we utter it, I really don't know. In that moment, I knew I was trying to gather my thoughts and feelings and find the words for my argument that I knew we would be having later.

Paul would have none of that. He turned in his seat to look at me and said, "You can't say that nothing is wrong. When I left the car, you were happy. I went into the store, got the five things you asked me to get and came back within minutes. I know you can't be upset with me since I did everything you asked. When you say nothing is wrong, I don't believe you. You can tell me now and we can get this over with, or you can hide it. We will show up to the party at odds with each other, ruin our night and then fight about ruining our night later. I prefer we just do this now."

Well, how is a gal supposed to respond to that?

In that moment I felt justified in my anger. My feelings started to turn grey. I believe we each have a dark place in our heart and in our head where even the most beautiful things, like being thankful for a loving husband who gives amazing gifts can turn ugly by sin. Allowing your feelings to have thoughts, will often lead to disaster. This is the only way to describe what went on in my head at this point.

I claimed my right to be upset and said, "If you must know, I am really hurt that you didn't buy me flowers. It would be nice to get flowers every now and then simply because you love me."

The truth is I don't even like getting flowers. I believe there are better things to spend your money on.

Paul knew this.

I knew Paul knew this.

Paul knew, I knew that he knew this.

Knowing this about me, Paul doesn't get me flowers. It's our thing. He still buys me little token's and surprises me with them, but never with flowers. This started back when we were dating. On our first date, Paul showed up at my door, hands behind his back. He smiled shyly at me and said, "I was going to get you flowers, so I got you this instead." He then handed me a Braeburn apple. He explained that this type of apple is his favorite to draw and he wanted to share a part of himself with me. Paul was an art major in college and Braeburn apples are a mix of green and red tones that make still life drawing more interesting. About a month later, he showed up for our date, gave me his famous line and handed me a Wonka bar. He remembered I was in the production of Charlie and the Chocolate Factory back in High School. Small tokens like these marked our dating life revealing how much he listened to me. In the end, that line was delivered with a diamond ring and a husband. Flowers have never been our thing, which makes this story, and my dark place, even more ridiculous.

I didn't think it was wrong for a girl to want flowers.

I didn't think it was wrong for me to desire token's of my husband's undying love for me.

I felt right in my mistreatment and stood my ground.

I watched as anger replaced the confusion on his face from before. I knew then this was going to be a real, big, drawn-out fight. I knew he was frustrated and angry with me. He was telling me all the ways that my argument was wrong, but I didn't hear him. I was too busy formulating my response.

That was until he said, "On the day we stood in front of God and family and friends, I made a promise to love you better than anyone else. You gave me the job of taking care of you and loving you. To see what you need and help provide for you. It's not fair for you to dictate how I love you. You just need to trust me to love you. So

back off and let me do my job!"

How's a gal to respond to that?

So here's the point. The moral of the story if you will:

>Unarticulated expectations can keep us from love.

But there's more than a moral...

Henry: Years ago, when Paul made that promise to Dani, I was there. I was younger then but I can still vouch that it happened. On that special day, I had front row privileges, for I was the ringbearer.

It was a great day of watching and supporting friends as they exchanged vows and the rings which I proudly walked down the aisle bearing on my little pillow while wearing a tuxedo with my pant leg tucked into a sock. But, it wasn't just a great day, it was a great weekend celebrating love, commitment and family. A weekend full of reconnecting with old friends and rehashing old memories. I can't tell you how many times I heard, "Hey do you remember when?" It was also a weekend full of new friends and new memories.

The weekend Paul made his promise to "do his job," was great because it was filled with expectancy, but we had no unarticulated expectations.

Before we dig into unarticulated expectations, I hope that you've digested the concept of repent as "thinking different after." It is only after we understand repent in the way it was originally used, that we can rightly begin to embrace the link between repent and forgive. We had to come to a new understanding when talking about *hamartia* and *metanoia*. Likewise, we must dive into *aphiemi*, the word that is translated "forgive" in the Bible.

Forgive is another one of those words that American's have loaded all kinds of baggage onto. To get this conversation started, let's take on our reactions to what I think is one of the most pervasive, yet mythical lines about forgiveness: "To forgive is to forget."

Dani: The day Paul and I got married was one of happiest days of my life, even when so many things went wrong. At one point, I was standing in my living room when the florist showed up with my bouquet. At first glance, I thought she was bringing me the throw away bouquet, to toss to the gals during the reception, but it wasn't. I am not a flower snob by any means, but when she gave me a plastic handle stuffed to the brim with pink carnations and a few red roses, I was speechless. Sure, I forgave her; but what she gave me was so far from what I told her I wanted.

I couldn't understand the miscommunication.

We ripped up all the flowers my father had paid for and added them to the flower girl basket to be tossed on the ground and walked upon. The girls and I ended up carrying fake flowers we pulled from my mother's dining room table center piece.

There are experiences, like this one that I don't want to forget because what happened shaped me, even if it was hard and was difficult to learn from. I forgave the florist years ago, I don't hold a grudge; but I haven't forgotten either. The truth is, I don't want to. I think back on that day a lot when I am trying to communicate clearly with other people. I want to make sure I don't repeat the same mistake. Jean Vanier says it this way,

> It is not a question of rejecting the past but of letting the past flow into the present and letting this process guide us as to how to live in the future.[2]

In order to repent we must remember the experience that is calling us to change the way we live. This muddies the water when looking at how repent and forgive fit together. This was a small moment of miscommunication, but there are other moments that hit deeper in our spirit. It's the moments[3] that are full of pain or joy when you realize that things should be different. That is the moment I want to hold on to because it teaches me what I want and need. I

shouldn't and wouldn't want to forget, I need to remember.

In Haiti there is a saying that I claim as my own, *"Pa pase Anba pye sa blye."* This means, "Do not pass under the forgetting tree." It's a beautiful way that parents and friends communicate with each other when someone leaves their village. Most often it is when children are sent into the city to be cared for by other family members, or parents have to give their kids up for adoption because caring for them is no longer financially possible.

Do not pass under the forgetting tree.

Do not forget where you come from, and who you are.

Do not forget the family you left behind.

There is even a tree planted by the airport in Port au Prince to remind visitors and natives alike, not to forget the people of Haiti. It begs of us not to forget their pain and suffering. The same is true for experiences we have in our lives that hold the power to teach us, changes us, guide us, and spur us on toward greater understanding and compassion.

We cannot forget.

We must not pass under the forgetting tree.

Henry: Forgiving and forgetting being closely linked together is a myth; but, there are all kinds of apocryphal tales that reinforce that myth. I've been forwarded variations of this one in several emails:

A woman went to her priest claiming that God was talking to her in a dream. When she explained that God told her the church should be operating in a certain way, and her priest was leery. Experience had taught him that people were not above concocting an idea themselves and then decided to use "dream" and "God" language as a trump card. This kind of manipulation had proven itself problematic and dangerous.

While pondering how to diffuse the situation, he remembered that just before this woman had walked into his office, he had visited with his Father Confessor. Under the pastoral seal he confessed his sins and received absolution for them. This seal was sacred. He knew his Father Confessor would never divulge his sins to another soul and he was certain that no one else, other than God Himself, had heard his confession. So he devised a test of sorts.

The priest explained that he wanted to be certain that her dream was from the Lord, and not merely a dream. He explained he had just returned from confession. Then he instructed her that the next time God appeared in a dream, she was to ask Him only one question. The answer would reveal to her if God was really talking to her, or if it was merely a dream about God. Only God would know the answer to this question. The woman was to ask what the sins were that the priest had just confessed.

The very next day, the woman bound into her priests study and exclaimed that God had spoken to her in a dream again.

"Did you ask which sins I had confessed yesterday?" the priest inquired.

"Certainly" she replied.

"What was the response of our Lord?" he asked.

She replied, "He said 'I don't remember.'"

The priest stood amazed. God had spoken to this woman.

> I, even I, am He who blots out your transgressions for my own sake, and remembers your sins no more.
> - Isaiah 43:25

I understand why an email like this gets the kind of traction it does. I believe in the power of story and you can see how a story like this reinforces the myth "to forgive is to forget." It wasn't until the last time I received this email, that the text from Isaiah was attached to the end. This doesn't just support the myth, it makes it seem biblical.

Reinforcing the false idea heaps guilt and shame on my shoulders because when someone does wrong to me and hurts me, try as I may I can't forget it. The healed wound leaves a tender spot and when that gets poked, I remember the pain.

Dani: The lofty standard that holds you accountable to forgiving and forgetting, assumes that you can reach a level of humanity that is impossible. I understand Henry's shame because I cannot achieve this level of forgetting, and so I then struggle with guilt.

Outside of this myth, forgetfulness is seen as a weakness. When we start forgetting things, we recognize that something is wrong. I think about the elderly people that I know. I see the signs that their brain isn't working the way it should and it signals that their body is breaking down. When I forget something someone told me, I immediately own the responsibility that I have fallen short.

If we believe the myth and support it with a misunderstanding of the verse from Isaiah, then we are presented with a God who by definition is defective. He automatically becomes either broken with his forgetfulness, or He is a liar. However, when we see Him as a God who chooses not to remember, He becomes again the God I know. A God full of compassion, and forgiveness, and love. It becomes His choice to let go of the things I have done wrong. This distinction in His character is critical to understanding who He is and the role He plays in our life.

God does forgive, but He does not forget.

Henry: We do not have a forgetful God. He's neither too busy nor is time taking it's toll on Him. This is a really good thing. At first blush it may seems that forgetting our sins would be a good thing, but if God could forget sins, what else could He forget? I've visited men and women with dementia and alzheimer's who have forgotten their spouse or children. If God were forgetful could He forget that we are His children?

As a child I wondered, "If to forgive is to forget, can I forget I forgave?" Could God actually forget that He forgave? Flipping the phrase like that not only illuminates the problem with the forgive and forget myth, but it begins to shine a light on the solution.

To make things very clear, the Bible teaches that through Jesus God forgives; but, it never says God forgets. When we read Isaiah 43:25, we notice it says that God does not remember. Not remembering is very different than forgetting. In fact many Hebrew scholars think the first word in verse 26, which is *"hazkire"*, belongs at the end of verse 25. This would make the verse end "remember not to remember." In fact, this cannot be more different that forgetting.

When we dispel the "forgive and forget" myth, we can look at what forgive really means. The word Jesus used, that we translate "forgive," is *aphiemi*. This word actually means "send away" or "leave behind."

In Matthew 4:11 after the Devil had tempted Jesus, it says that "Then the devil *aphiemi*" Jesus. The devil forgave Jesus? No, at least not the way most of us have been taught to think about forgive. We say, "the devil left Jesus." Likewise, in Mark 1:18 the disciples "*aphiemi* their nets and followed" Jesus. Would anybody think the disciples had to forgive these nets? I've never seen a translation, and never will, that says they did anything with their nets other than leave them behind. They dropped them on the shore and walked away.

This is the point.

To not forgive means we hold onto something, stay with it, and carry it around. To forgive means we drop it, leave it behind and refuse to carry it any longer.

Dani: Finding the true meaning behind the words we use every day can be an incredibly freeing exercise. It changes the story and shapes the way we view ourselves, our relationships and our belief in God. When I really start to live out repentance in a way that helps me to think differently after, I am more able to forgive and to

let go of the hurt that holds me back.

We do ourselves a disservice when we do not fully allow repentance to penetrate our way of thinking. We form habits in the way we repeat certain behaviors. When I do not think differently after, I am condemned to remain stagnant as a person, unable to let go of the baggage I bring with me, instead of letting go of the hurt that holds me back.

It is really hard to share the story of my expectations of receiving flowers from Paul that day because of how immaturely I reacted. However, this small moment in my marriage taught me so much about myself as well as my relationships. That day, I was faced with an opportunity to repent. I could take that moment of insecurity and either stay in that mindset, creating a division in my marriage, or I could own my behavior and choose differently the next time. If I chose to repent, I would need to accept my own forgiveness and let it go, and also trust my husband's forgiveness and that he would let it go.

The other piece in this story is what happened in those five minutes of my daydreaming: I had formed an expectation of how Paul would behave.

Henry: When we say expectations, we are talking about unarticulated expectations. We say "I love you man," "I love my wife," and "I love burritos." The word love is the same but the concepts are very different. Even when I say, "I love my wife," my experience of spousal love is likely different than yours. I was working with a young lady whose husband was abusive; yet, he claimed, "I hit you because I love you." Even after she left the relationship and got to a safe place, conversations about spousal love were difficult because of her experience. Yet, the unease of these conversations pailed in comparison to their value; for they brought with them heavenly meaning. Likewise, conversations about expectations are uncomfortable and at times confusing; but they are essential for they to can usher in heavenly meaning.

Dani: Just like the word love has many different meanings, the same is true for expectations. This word is often used in hindsight by people when they are describing their hopes and wants and desires. When we look back at the moral, we aim to specifically understand unarticulated expectations. These unspoken hopes have a sneaky and conniving way that steals the love out of our relationships. They hide behind more innocuous concepts but can not be met.

I had an expectation of the way Paul should behave. This form of expectation is not uncommon. We want others to read our mind and know our desires. Then when they don't and we are disappointed, we blame them. We think, "You didn't behave correctly, so now I am angry." Living in these types of expectations holds the power to damage relationships because of the hurt it creates.

The damage comes when we shut down and keep the other person at a distance from our thoughts or feelings. When I am hurting, I often need time to process what is going on. I need space to figure out how I am feeling. We talked about this type of artistic space. The damage from shutting down comes when I shut people out long after I know how I feel. Needing the right amount of time can help me to figure things out, but too much time isolates me from the people in my life. The difficulty in shutting down is that it says, "You hurt me, so I won't trust you anymore." There is no room for forgiving or repenting. It is important to understand the balance between artistic space and shutting down.

Henry: As we create healthy artistic space and learn to repent, we choose who, what, and when to forgive. We will begin to see that expectations are always *hamartia* and need to be forgiven.

Unarticulated expectations live in our minds and even speaking them has an effect on them. This is how it is with much of life. Once at a prayer meeting, Mick Woodhead, challenged us to all

pray aloud at the same time. We were not to concern ourselves with listening to anyone else's prayer but our own. "Your ears need to hear, what your mouth is saying and your mind is thinking," he said.

I was amazed at the way hearing my thoughts spoken affected me.

One of the first ways we can forgive expectations is by saying them. When we say something we are sending it away from existing only in our mind. I'm amazed at how rarely I hear people articulate expectations. In the few cases I've heard "I expect you to do this or that," the person saying it has significant power over the one they are saying it to. It seems that person, rather than owning the fact that they have that much power, and just telling the other person to do something, uses the word "expect." Expect seems a bit softer, unless the expectation isn't met.

For example, a teacher will say to a group of preschool students, "I expect you to keep your hands to yourself." This is not a desire or a hope, and though the word "expect" is used, it's not an expectation either. It is a demand. At first blush, that word may seem a little harsh, and perhaps we default to expectation simply to soften the demand; but if the child does not keep their hands to themselves, they will be punished. That is why I call it a demand. If there are two people who are on an equal playing field, you will never hear one say to the other, "I expect." Can you even imagine Dani saying to Paul, "I expect you to buy me flowers?"

Once an expectation is expressed it morphs and changes. As Dani has articulated her expectation of flowers, she came to realize she never really wanted them in the first place. Dani said, "Expectations can be tricky because they hide behind words like 'hope' or 'want' or 'desire.'"

Expectations hide behind these things by never being expressed, because expressing them, sending them out of our minds and mouths and into the ear of another is an experiment in T.R.U.S.T. If I tell you my desire, my hope, or something I want, you can reject it and this can be scary.

Dani: While expectations limit to specific possibilities that only exists in your head; expectancy opens oneself up. Expectancy is learning to live in T.R.U.S.T of another. Expectancy builds upon a general belief and hope in the character of someone else.

Healthy communication is the point of inflection between expectations and expectancy. Part of effective communication is a strong self-awareness. It is the ability to understand your own limits, needs and wants, and to be able to communicate those to the people in your life.

Henry: Repentance allows us to unpack our expectations into conversations about hopes and dreams. As we do this, we develop an environment of expectancy where others are aware of our deepest desires. Inasmuch we are open to great things happening, rather than being discontent if a specific expectation goes unmet. We are inviting others to the table to live more than a story with us.

If Dani held onto expectations regarding the flowers that day in the car, rather than living in the expectancy of trusting Paul to love her as he promised to, she might have missed her 30th birthday, the epitome of expectancy.

Dani: Paul knows me better than anyone. He knows when I am lying, when I am struggling, and when I need something. That is the result of over communicating and living in expectancy. For my 30th Birthday, I was taking the kids to Michigan for a two week vacation to visit my family. Since Paul can't take that much time off of work, he couldn't come with us. When everyone kept asking what I wanted for my birthday, I simply replied, "I would love enough money to buy my husband a plane ticket so he can come for a long weekend and have a vacation with us."

Paul thought this was strange. He asked, "For your birthday, you want to buy me a ticket so I can go on vacation?"

"Yes." I replied.

"So... you are essentially buying me for your birthday?" Leave it to him to make it sound creepy.

A few weeks later, the kids and I made it to Michigan and Paul was able to join us for a long weekend. On the trip out, his plane was delayed. He ended up not getting to my folks house until well after one o'clock in the morning. For him it was a long day of work and travel, so when my alarm went off at 5:45 to go for my morning run, I tried hard not to wake him. I moved quietly around the room gathering my running shoes and shorts and then I heard him stir. I whispered for him to go back to sleep. He crawled out of bed, turned around and said, "If you are going running, I am going with you. You bought me this weekend, so I am spending all my time with you."

I didn't know what to say to that.

My husband is athletic, but not the type that wakes up only after a handful of hours of sleep to go run four miles. I am ashamed to admit, that while I loved this attention, my first fleeting thought was, "Man, I hope he doesn't slow me down."

Once we were out the door, we jogged and enjoyed each other's company a great deal. When we returned to my folk's house, everyone was still sleeping, so we stayed outside, stretching and resting. Before he even sat down, Paul asked if he could get me some water.

I started to notice how the whole weekend was playing out this way. As a mom, I generally eat last. I am often inhaling cold food before I am needed again. I noticed though that multiple times that weekend, I was sitting and eating a hot meal with other adults while Paul got the kids food and took care of all of their needs.

By the evening of the fourth of July, we were all waiting out on the boat to go see the fireworks. Everyone was accounted for except

Paul. After a few moments, he strolled out of the house with his pinstripe suit on, tie and all. He stood out compared to the rest of us who were donning our pajamas. I asked him what was going on and he simply said, "This is your favorite outfit of mine, so I thought I would wear it for you." At that point, I couldn't take it anymore. I asked him what was going on.

"I know how much you are always taking care of everyone all the time. I thought for your birthday, I could serve you. I didn't want to tell you about it, I just wanted to do it and let you enjoy someone else taking care of you for a change. I know acts of service are your strongest love language and so I decided to make sure I served you all weekend."

That's what I got for my birthday.

I don't like flowers, but I will take you washing my dishes any day of the week. Paul knows this about me. He knows what reaches into my heart and speaks love to me. This is what trusting his character and living into expectancy of his love for me looks like.

Silently expecting him to behave a certain way got us nowhere but frustrated, disappointed, and tense. That's what unarticulated expectations do.

He proved to me again that weekend that I can trust him to know me and that I can sit back and let him do his job.

The beauty in that is how much it revealed to me about the way God loves me. How I can learn to trust Him and sit back and let Him do His job, instead of telling God how it should be done. I can trust God's character because He has proven to be trustworthy and He doesn't forget.

CHAPTER 12:

Candles, Cake, Cocaine

~by Dani

Birthdays are a really big deal in my family. My mother claimed that since we all had to share the holidays, your birthday was the one day set aside just for you. A day set apart to cherish and appreciate the gift of your life. It's nice having someone in your family who loves celebrating your life.

Growing up in my home, the morning of your birthday you would be greeted by signs hung throughout the house. Signs that read, "Happy Birthday!" or "You are special" or even better, "No one else is like you!" These signs were hung everywhere: in the refrigerator, attached to the milk carton and in the bathroom, taped to the underside of the toilet seat. The birthday signs were the first thing you saw in the morning and the last thing you noticed before bed. If that didn't make you feel special, my mom made it her personal mission to hug you and say "I love you" as many times as are humanly possible in one day. Growing up with her was awesome!

The best tradition however was that the birthday person got to select which restaurant to eat at that night. Being a family on a limited income, we ate out only five times a year: once on each of our birthdays.

It was February 5, my dad's birthday, and even though I was only 10 years old, I remember this birthday more than any other. My dad always worked the midnight shift on the police force. He started work at midnight then drove me to school at 7:30 a.m. Each morning he was finished by 8:00 a.m., and in bed by 8:30 a.m. This day was different because my dad was helping in a major drug stake out.

Through the course of drug users ratting out their dealers, Detroit was looking at their largest international drug bust to date. They had a string of informants that gave up the names and locations of some of the biggest distributors between Detroit, Michigan and Windsor, Canada. My father's shift in the stakeout was scheduled from 8:00 a.m. in the morning until 4:00 in the afternoon. The plan was that after we came home from school, and my dad's shift was over, we would meet at the house then go out to supper.

By 4:00 p.m., everyone was home except dad. This wasn't highly unusual with his career so we continued to wait on him, doing homework and watching "The Cosby Show" to pass the time.

4:30 p.m. came and went.

5:30 p.m. came and went.

We watched an episode of "Who's the Boss" and it was now after 6:00 p.m.

Still no dad.

At this point, I am convinced that most families would worry. But not us. Nothing bad had ever happened to our dad before. He was still invincible in our mind's eyes. Nothing could hurt him. The only thing we were consumed with was irritation at how hungry we were getting. This was one of those moments that we didn't like my dad's job. You never knew when he would be kept away.

Around 6:30 that evening, two and a half hours after he was supposed to be home, he finally called.

We overheard mom talking to him. After almost a full day stake out, they had made the bust. They caught the bad guys, but were now left with a semi truck full of cocaine and marijuana. It was now considered evidence, so my father and the other officers needed to take the three pallets of drugs to the warehouse and do inventory. I heard my dad explain that he would be there most of the night. We would need to reschedule his birthday dinner celebration.

My brother, and sister, and I were all really bummed. My mom however, was determined. Her love of birthdays was only surpassed by her love for my dad, which stirred an idea in her head. When she hung up the phone, she told us all to go get our shoes on. We were going out.

My mom piled the three of us in the car. She packed the festive helium balloons, my dad's birthday present and the homemade cake decorated with love. Then we headed for the warehouse. If my dad couldn't make it to his birthday celebration, well then that celebration was going to make it to my dad.

After a short drive, we arrived at the warehouse and got out of the car. Mom starting filling each of our hands. My sister was first in line carrying the balloons. Then there was me balancing the cake hoping not to drop it while I walked. My brother followed up carrying the present.

My mother was determined to celebrate the life of the man she loved more than anything.

Shivering out in the cold in the beginning of February, mom lit the candles on the cake. She quietly swung open the door, looked at us and in a whispered demand, told us to start singing.

"Happy Birthday to you. Happy Birthday to you. Happy Birthday to dad…Happy Birthday to you."

We hadn't made to the back of the warehouse yet. So we were told to just keep singing.

"Happy Birthday to…" I became incredibly distracted by all the "evidence" in the warehouse. As we sang, my eyes were glued to shelf after shelf of radios, weapons, computers, TVs, you name it. It was all tagged, labeled and telling a story I couldn't fully comprehend.

After walking through the dark aisles of police evidence, there they were: five police officers still wearing Kevlar, surrounded by three walls of drugs. Each wall was neatly packed, wrapped in cellophane and stood at least 10 feet high.

I couldn't believe my eyes.

All three of us had stopped singing, too stunned to continue.

To say the least, the officers were surprised to see us. The excitement and pure joy on the face of my dad was exactly what my mother was hoping for. After hugging my mother, he came over, blew out the candles, and gave each of us a kiss for making his day better.

As you can imagine, the evidence warehouse isn't known for hosting Birthday parties and gatherings. The officers started arranging barrels of cocaine around in a circle to provide somewhere to sit. We cut into the cake, each pulling up a stack of drugs to get comfortable on. We laughed at the irony of what we were sitting on and took fun pictures. The officers recounted their adventures of the stake out that day as we watched my dad open his presents.

Reality set in and the amount of work the police still needed to get to moved them to clear away the plates and left over cake. The story telling and laughs continued as pounds of cocaine got hoisted onto their shoulders and stored away on shelves. It was a birthday we would never forget.

So here's the point. The moral of the story if you will:

> Sometimes a story happens to you.
> Sometimes you've got to happen to the story.

But there's more than a moral...

Henry: I was lucky to be raised in a storytelling family. Being born in New York to an Italian family on my mothers side, for better or for worse all the stereotypes rang true. Dinners were pasta based and plentiful and the stories flowed as freely as the vino.

Food and family played such a huge roll in my childhood that when we left the extended family of aunts and uncles, cousins and grandparents in New York, so we had to create one.[1] Even though we had moved halfway across the country, meals were still a big deal in my family and Thanksgiving was the biggest meal of the year. That first year in Colorado is the Thanksgiving I remember most vividly and fondly. We lived in a single wide trailer and the place was packed. Even though it was snowing outside, we had to

keep every window and door open and people were still sweating. We drug a couple sawhorses inside and put pieces of plywood on top, creating a makeshift table just to hold all the desserts. Friends brought beverages which they stuck right in the snowbank to keep cool. I was intrigued with Steve, a guy my dad worked with, who arrived on his cross country skis and brought a leather bota filled with wine.

That Thanksgiving was memorable not only for the packed house and plentiful food, but because it was also the night I became a storyteller.

I had just started kindergarten and was fake-reading a joke book I'd checked out of the school library for the long weekend. I say fake-read because I could barely sound out the words. I had attempted to sound out the first word and by the second became bored of the process. So, taking the word or two that I knew I would hypothesize the rest of the sentence, being certain that at least my inflection made it funny.

Steve took interest in my giggling and "reading" aloud as I wiggled on my beanbag chair. Amused, he struck up a conversation and asked what was so funny. I told him a joke or two and he actually laughed. Since he laughed, I must have been funny so I became louder and more animated. As I did, he grabbed a high back bar stool that we had borrowed from my dad's restaurant, picked me up and put me on top of it. I grasped the back of the stool with one hand and my joke book with the other. Holding my stool so my wiggling wouldn't tip it over, he shouted, "Quiet down, little Henry has something to say."

So I cleared my throat and made up a few jokes. These were my very first funny stories.

Steve started clapping and others joined in. Since I was the hosts' kids, everyone gave a socially kind laugh, and the party went on. People returned to their food, and their drink and sharing their own stories. Steve was a bachelor and his attention quickly moved to one of the ladies at the party. He refilled her wine from his leather bota and I overheard him telling her a funny story about when he was a kid, like me. I thought my silly jokes had inspired his story, maybe they did; but at that point, as a very young boy I started to see the power of storytelling.

Dani: Henry and I both saw great stories at a young age. I started to recognize a good story when my dad would talk about work as a police officer. His job almost required that he not only collect good stories, but that he would live them. He had the ability to mesmerize an audience with his tales from the streets. I remember watching how his entire demeanor changed, his voice got louder, and he commanded attention. Everyone sat enthralled as he wove his stories of bad guys and justice.

I can only remember one time that my dad got injured on the job. When we showed up to a large family birthday party, everyone gathered around while he told about the guy who busted his face and almost broke his nose.

My dad started recounting the story of a car chase. After the perpetrator found himself trapped in an alley, he got out of his car. He ran toward the dark alley, blocked off with a high gate. My dad threw his car in park and got out to chase after him. The guy made it over the fence and was followed closely by my dad. Dad was animated while he talked and I looked around, watching everyone watch him. I even noticed that people in other conversations started to listen in. He had drawn the attention of everyone in the room.

The man being chased started to scale the next fence in the alley. My dad was right behind him, climbing, almost reaching him to drag him down. The perpetrator turned and in a split second, kicked my dad in the face, with him ultimately falling to the ground gripping his nose as blood dripped to the cement. With pain filling his eyes, my dad pulled himself back up. Anger fueled his commitment to

scaling the fence and running full speed after his target.

The room was quiet as everyone hung on every word my dad said. You could see the sparkle in his eye behind the black and blue bruises. He was reliving it and telling the story in such a way that everyone in the room felt like they were there.

The target made it to a low fence at the end of the alley. My dad had gained on him once again, and in an effort to not repeat his previous mistake of climbing after the guy, adrenaline kicked in, and my dad hurled himself over the fence to land on top of the guy on the other side. He had his target pinned to the ground. His eyes were blurring as they swelled, his nose most likely broken, blood everywhere, perpetrator caught. The story finished, the room was silent. Everyone was enchanted. It was then that I realized the power of telling a good story.

Henry: We have all had days where things go wrong and plans get ruined. Most of these days don't turn out to be good stories. I can remember evenings when my mom cooked a really good dinner and dad ended up having to work late. We all ate without him.

The story of my dad being late just happened to us; nobody happened to the story. But on Dani's dad's birthday Dani's mom wasn't willing to just let the story happen - she made a choice to happen to the story.

Dani: My mother loves making memories. This phrase is her philosophy for life: "Time to make memories." I remember one summer when I was a child I was invited to attend camp with some friends. I didn't feel like hanging out and playing games and staying up late. Normally those were things I loved doing, but this time I wanted nothing to do with it. I was in the middle of a good book and I just wanted to stay home. I talked to my mom about this and she told me, "Sometimes you have to do things you don't want to do. Sometimes you realize that it is important to be with people, to participate, and force yourself to have fun. When you show up and do something that you didn't feel like doing, you will usually be blessed with great memories with friends. If you go and show up, most of the time you end up having a lot of fun."

She would encourage me to look at why I didn't want to participate in making memories or great stories. Most of the time, it didn't matter why I didn't want to do it, she would tell me I should just show up and see the gift I would receive in participating. Looking back, I can see how right she was. I notice how often I hold those words up to my life now and push myself to show up, even when I don't feel like it. I understand that life is lived in community, and not in the isolation of solitude.

When we actively decide to participate in the stories happening around us, we start to collect memories.

Henry: So many of my childhood stories revolve around Church. We didn't just go on Sunday mornings, we hung around in the church basement for games and meals throughout the week. Mom and Dad sacrificed so that my siblings and I could attend a Christian grade school. During the summer, I loved going to Church Camp and not just because it's where I had my first slow dance.

Although I've got so many great memories or Church, I've also spent more than my fair share of time questioning if Christianity was really for me. I spent so much time and energy checking out other philosophies and religions that my advisor at Ball State had me declare Religious Studies as my major. The thing that keeps bringing me back to Christianity though, is simply grace.

Today, Christianity is my full time gig. Promise lets me be their Pastor, and if you ever visited us (yes, that is an invitation[2]), I hope you walked away experiencing grace. If we had a theme verse it would be,

> For it is by grace you have been saved, through faith—and this is not from yourselves, it is the gift of God— not by works, so that no one can boast.[3]

The fact that I have even one pair that sticks by my side, through all the bull, helping me to live *more than a story* is pure grace. When I think about grace more and wrestle with the fact that the God who created the universe madly, deeply, passionately, perfectly and purely loves me, it still blows my mind.

I learned of grace at my darkest hour through *The Raggamuffin Gospel*,[4] perhaps the greatest book on grace ever written, but certainly the best one I've ever read. I wept even reading his introduction:

> The Ragamuffin Gospel was written with a specific reading audience in mind.
>
> This book is not for the super spiritual.
>
> It is not for muscular Christians who have made John Wayne, and not Jesus, their hero.
>
> It is not for academics who would imprison Jesus in the ivory tower of exegisis.
>
> It is not for noisy, feel-good folks who manipulate Christianity into a naked appeal to emotion.
>
> It is not for hooded mystics who want magic in their religion.
>
> It is not for Alleluia Christians who live only on the mountaintop and have never visited the valley of desolation.
>
> It is not for the fearless and tearless.
>
> It is not for red-hot zealots who boast with the rich young ruler of the Gospels, "All these commandments I have kept from my youth."
>
> It is not for the complacent who hoist over their shoulders a tote bag of honors, diplomas, and good works, actually believing they have it made.
>
> It is not for legalists who would rather surrender control of their souls to rules than run the risk of living in union

with Jesus.

If anyone is still reading along, it was written for the bedraggled, beat-up, and burnt-out.

It is for the sorely burdened who are still shifting the heavy suitcase from one hand to the other.

It is for the wobbly and weak-kneed who know they don't have it all together and are too proud to accept the handout of amazing grace.

It is for inconsistent, unsteady disciples whose cheese is falling off their cracker.

It is for poor, weak, sinful men and women with hereditary faults and limited talents.

It is for earthen vessels who shuffle along on feet of clay.

It is for the bent and the bruised who feel that their lives are a grave disappointment to God.

It is for smart people who know they are stupid and honest disciples who admit they are scallywags.

It is a book I wrote for myself and anyone who has grown weary and discouraged along the Way.

I wondered if Manning had hidden cameras at my place, for I had attempted to be all those for whom his book hadn't been written and only recently admitted I was all those for whom he had. I can't understate how committed I am to grace as an unearned, unmerited free gift[4] and nothing else.

This is one of the reasons I'm not a huge fan of the Santa Claus myth. While Saint Nick is one of my favorite early church fathers for all kinds of reasons,[5] giving gifts to good little boys and girls confuses grace. I know I'm pushing into a sensitive topic here. I realized that that the day Tricia and I got a call from the preschool superintendent where our daughter Kaitlyn was enrolled.

We never told our kids Santa was real. I made that decision long before I met my wife and lucky for me she agreed. So Tricia and I were honest with our kids. We told them about Saint Nick and that many people pretended that Santa brought gifts on Christmas morning as a way to remember the great things he did. Since Kaitlyn understood pretending and games, it was still fun. It also meant that when she got really excited about a gift she wouldn't look to the sky and exclaim "Thank you Santa!" rather her mom and I would get all the hugs, affection, and credit.

The biggest reason we avoided the Santa myth is because it really muddies the waters of grace. The basic concept is the separation of naughty kids and nice kids, those who do good things and those who do bad things. The kids who do bad things get coal (which really never happens) and the kids that do good things get gifts. That is the problem, if you have to do something for it then it's not a gift. A gift is the key concept of grace, and Santa says you have to do something to earn it.

Since Jesus, whose birth we celebrate at Christmas, is the ultimate free gift, I don't ever want someone to think they have to do something to earn Him or His love.

I guess I explained this pretty clearly to Kaitlyn because when the school superintendent called, she told me that is exactly what Kaitlyn had explained to the other preschooler on the playground. While the superintendent agreed with my explanation, she still insisted that Kaitlyn "play along" a bit more.

"She has such a big heart and I know she really was concerned for this little girl," the teacher explained. Kaitlyn caused some issues in expressing her concern, especially when she exclaimed, "I'm calling the cops because your parents are lying to you and that's against the law."

I'll admit, we needed to work on tact a bit, and explain what was was illegal; but we didn't have to explain the difference between a wage and a free gift, so maybe it was worth it.

At times we hesitate to talk about the things we do or the way we happen to a story. It would be intellectually dishonest to affirm my belief in grace and at the same time claim that I can do something - anything - to earn my salvation, because there is a huge difference between a wage and a gift.

Dani: When I think about a wage versus a gift I am struck not only by how I approach my faith, but also how I approach my life. Wage speaks to a "doing" attitude, while "gift" resembles a "being" attitude.

I would like to say that I live out my faith as a gift, but I know deep down that it slips back into being a wage I want to earn. This language is healthy to keep fresh in my mind to hold my actions accountable. Scripture says, "For the wages of sin is death, but the gift of God is eternal life through Jesus Christ our Lord."[6] I have earned death through my sins, but there is absolutely nothing I can do to earn my salvation. It is a gift. Whether I have been good or bad, it is mine. God, in his great mercy[7] showed compassion on me; he saw me in my brokenness and said, "I know you can't do this. I have what you need. Salvation, freedom, love, mercy and hope are yours. I give them to you because I love you."

God's power overcomes darkness and He is incapable of nothing. This power is ours because he has given it to us. The beauty in this gift, the freedom of being able to say yes to it, is that it is not dependent on us being good enough to get it or to lose it.

I believe that often we live our lives thinking we must choose, either – a "doing" attitude or a "being" attitude. But life doesn't exist within those boundaries. Most of life needs to be embraced in the philosophy of both/and rather than either/or. When I am talking with friends about personal issues and how I get to the point of being so stressed out, I start to list all the ways I may have gotten off course. Lack of sleep, poor eating habits, over commitment, lack of mediation or devotional time, and the list goes on. Once I see the

list, I am compelled to choose between my downfalls. Most often, if not always, the choice isn't either/or but it is a combination of all these things. It is not either lack of sleep or poor eating habits. Rather, the reason I am stressed out is because of both lack of sleep and poor eating habits. All things in life are interconnected; they cannot be separated. We as humans are made up of body, soul, mind and emotions. All of these things depend on one another and cannot be dealt with separately. You cannot choose either your physical health or your mental health. They both work together.

I talk about either/or and both/and because it speaks to a "doing" and "being" lifestyle. I think it is wonderful how God doesn't force us to choose. Life is a both/and world. We do not choose the gift, but we can choose to show up in our story with the gift that God has given us. We are both "being" people and "doing" people. I don't have to do anything to be a child of God. I can however, do everything because I am a child of God. He gave me the gift of "being" and I give the world my gift of "doing."

Henry: It's not just that you were saved from something, you were saved for something too. If we read only

> For it is by grace you have been saved, through faith—and this is not from yourselves, it is the gift of God— not by works, so that no one can boast.[8]

and stopped, we can easily slip into an either works, or grace mentality. The very next verse says this,

> For we are God's handiwork, created in Christ Jesus to do good works, which God prepared in advance for us to do.[9]

Did you catch that? It is a both/and concept. We were both saved by grace and saved for works. We are not just supposed to let the story happen; we are supposed to happen to the story.

Many who read, "happen to the story" read it as "make the story happen." That is a close enough reading for all practical purposes, but there is a subtle difference. If you or I are charged to make the story happen, that is a lot of pressure.

When I was a child and my parents were going through a divorce, I deeply and desperately wanted to make a different story happen, but I couldn't. Like many kids whose parents get divorced and who long to make a story happen, I was left with all kinds of false guilt. Even though everyone told me it wasn't my fault, I still wondered what I could have done to make it all different.

As I read the Bible verses above, this becomes very clear. We can only happen to the story. We can only do the good work that God prepared for us.

He gave us the tools; we just need to use them. We happen to the story, but everything has been prepared for us in advance. When Dani's mom found out what was going on, she didn't rush to make a cake, it was already there. She didn't fret about buying balloons and filling them with helium, she used what had been prepared in advance. She took what she already had and lived into the story.

Dani: So often we are waiting until we are ready. We say, "When I am older, I am going to _____. When I have enough money I am going to _____."

We leave the spaces empty, waiting and preparing to do that great thing, to live that amazing story, or to become the person we always dreamed we could be. The truth of the matter is that no one is ever ready. Most people living into their story, making dreams come true or creating memories, don't feel ready. They just knew they had to show up. I remember when I entered the world of blogging. It took me almost two years of indecision and doubt to overcome my fear of not feeling ready. I would scour other blogs and authors and become intimidated. I would compare my value and voice to others. I came away believing that I needed "more" before I could start. More wisdom, more experience, more education, or more insight; you name it. I chose not to live into this story because I didn't

feel prepared. Then one day something clicked inside of me and I realized that I could either live with regret, or I could show up.

God revealed to me that I had been ready because he was with me. The truth for me in this, is that humanity suffers when individuals don't show up for their life; when they spend their life trying to prepare for the story instead of just living.

CHAPTER 13:

~by Henry

Once upon a time, almost 50 years ago, there was a simple corner store in the little Italian neighborhood where my mother grew up. They sold all the basics that a New York community would need: milk and eggs, papers and penny candies. But on Saturdays, early in the morning, the proprietor would heat up the fryer and make doughnuts.

As all Junior High children do, my mother was getting more and more responsibility and one Saturday morning, her parents sent her to this corner store with the money to purchase a dozen doughnuts. After a short walk, she arrived and stood in line waiting to place her order. When she finally made her way up to the front of the line, the man behind the counter made some small talk and gave her attention, something all people, but especially teenagers crave.

After a bit more chit chat, my mom said, "I would like a dozen doughnuts please," and she paid the man.

He took her money, gave her some change, and then began to box up the doughnuts. Continuing the small talk he asked, "Do you know what a bakers dozen is?"

A smile crept across her face. Knowing the answer to a question is always a good thing, but when an expert in the field asks a question and you know the answer, it's downright exciting. So with a glimmer in her eye, my mother exclaimed, "A baker's dozen is 13 instead of 12."

The baker smiled back and put one extra doughnut on a piece of waxed paper, and placed it on top of the boxed dozen. "Since you knew, a baker's dozen it is," he said.

Mom took the box and as she walked home she enjoyed that one extra special treat.

So here's the point. The moral of the story if you will:

You'll never know where going the extra mile will take you.

But there's more than a moral...

Henry: It has surprised me how many people have said we shouldn't put 13 chapters in this book. They say it's bad luck. When I explain that I like the number 13, that it's the row I try to book when I fly; I always get the, "You're tempting fate" look. Sometimes, people even say it outright.

I became intrigued by this and found out that the fear of 13 is so pervasive that it even has a name.

Triskaidekaphobia.

With a name like that who couldn't take this fear seriously.

Still, I've never really understood it. Maybe the bakers dozen story that my mom told when I was a child just stuck with me. It's amazing which stories stick, embedding themselves in the memory, and which stories people quickly forget. My parents are always amazed to hear which stories my brothers, sister, and I recount in vivid detail when we gather at the table. Tricia and I are starting to have the same experience with our children. What we thought was a passing comment or a fleeting moment is an essential story to them. When my mom found out this story was in the book, she was surprised I even remembered it.

Mom didn't remember telling it, but it was important to me. Perhaps that story made such a positive link with the number 13 that I've never feared it. Let's face it - it's not just kids that get excited at the thought of free stuff (doughnuts included). Maybe I linked the number 13 with good fortune and free sweets.

I looked into this fear, wanting to understand where it came from, and found out that Italians in the old neighborhood and around the world consider 13 a lucky number. That is, except when sitting at the dinner table. Most say this has to do with Jesus, since He ate His last supper with 12 other people, 13 in all. But I think it has to do with our love for having good conversation around the table. People who study proxemics have discovered that when you move from 12 people to 13 people, the dynamics differ so much that the

groups are even given different names.[1] One of the most noticeable shifts is that once the group goes from 12 to 13, there are at least two conversations going on at the same time.

There are a lot of people who are afraid of 13 and there are all kinds of traditional reasons why:

13 steps up to the gallows and 13 turns in the hangman's noose.

13 witches in a coven.

Apollo 13.

On Spongebob Squarepants, children learn from Mr. Krabs that there are 13 dirty words.

And speaking of children we must remember the scariest 13 of all: when children become teenagers.

To me, the fear around the number 13 is silly. Some, like the thirteen club, set forth to debunk the fear and would sit 13 people around a table for dinner on the 13th of each month. If a member showed up late they were fined 13 cents.[2]

There is something to be said about fear and taking it on. Chester Arthur, Grover Cleveland (while he was president), Benjamin Harrison, William McKinley and Theodore Roosevelt all took on the fear of the number of 13 and are listed among the 400 members of the thirteen club. They also all went on to become President.

Dani: I could care less about the number 13. It doesn't scare me or threaten me. I never think twice about it. I don't understand this fear.

Then I take a moment and think about the things that I am afraid of:

I am terrified of heights.

I don't possess a whole lot of gracefulness, which in turn makes me very afraid of climbing bleachers or high ladders where I can fall.

I am afraid of my parents dying.

I am really afraid of being too scared to live my life fully, and subsequently having regrets about lacking the courage to live my story loudly and fully and with total abandon.

I am afraid of being a coward.

Like Triskaidekaphobia, these are irrational fears.

Living in a tough neighborhood where our home and car have been broken into multiple times, our family lives in a relative amount of fear. This fear is based in reality. I am no stranger to being afraid of people, of life, of my abilities and my brokenness. Fear is something I understand.

We can't judge each other for the fears we have. Some are grounded in experiences, and some are irrational. It is part of the baggage we carry. All humans are afraid of something. We all have fear. Here we find common ground and can relate to one another. We can empathize with the shared experience of being afraid.

Henry: When the topic of fear comes up, many people dismiss it with a quote President Franklin Roosevelt and say, "The only thing we have to fear is fear itself." While I'd gladly unpack this quote with a pair over coffee, I find this quote by President Teddy Roosevelt[3] who was a member of the thirteen club more beneficial to the discussion of fear.

It is not the critic who counts; not the man who points out how the strong man stumbles, or where the doer of deeds could have done them better. The credit belongs to the man who is actually in the arena, whose face is marred by dust and sweat and blood; who strives valiantly; who errs, who comes short again and again, because there is no effort without error and shortcoming; but who does actually strive to do the deeds; who knows great enthusiasms, the great devotions; who spends himself in a worthy cause; who at the best knows in the end the triumph of high achievement, and who at the worst, if he fails, at least fails while daring greatly, so that his

place shall never be with those cold and timid souls who neither know victory nor defeat.[4]

Some people will mock and patronize another's fear. These people will discount another's story rather than being part of a pair. So often, people tell me a story that they have never told anyone else because they are afraid it isn't enough. They are afraid of the critic who will point out a weakness. This is bad, but what is even worse is when someone chooses not to "happen to the story" because they are afraid.

Dani: Fear is hard to combat because it is unseen and lives in our mind. It is a war that exists in our brains, unseen by others, rendering it easy to deny. It can stay hidden and tucked away, never surfacing to be confronted or comforted by others. Scripture is scattered with many encouragements regarding fear and how to fight it with courage.

Isaiah 41:10 says,

> So do not fear, for I am with you; do not be dismayed, for I am your God. I will strengthen you and help you; I will uphold you with my righteous right hand.

Fear is a prison that keeps us from honesty, truth, and self worth. It keeps us locked up often from even living out our lives. I lived in fear for more than five years believing I wasn't capable, or good enough, or knowledgeable enough to be an inspirational speaker. I was afraid that people might not like me, or that I would be terrible at it. I was afraid I wouldn't be the best. That I would never be able to say out loud that I had this dream. If I said it out loud, then I might have to do something about it. If I told people, they could laugh at me, discourage me, or my greatest fear of all; tell me to my face that I would be great while privately believing the opposite. I was afraid I would never know the truth.

Sometimes the fear of our story is never about a dream, but a reality we have experienced. It is a story that has already happened

to us. We have already been hurt and we are afraid that if people knew, they would view us different, or they wouldn't believe us, or they would judge us for what happened. We wonder if the risk of telling our story is worth the chance of being hurt again. The fear of admitting that part of your life, your story, can keep you from experiencing the fullness of community. A life without community is never fruitful. Even more than missing out on the benefits of community, your life will always be partly hidden because fear will make sure you never tell anyone.

God reassures us in this fear when he writes, "Have I not commanded you? Be strong and courageous. Do not be afraid; do not be discouraged, for the Lord your God will be with you wherever you go."[5]

We are not left alone in our insecurity, our unmet dreams, and our failed attempts of living a great story. We are not left alone in our fear, for God promises to be with us. When He invited us to live the story of our life, He never intended for us to be alone. His desire is to walk with us each step of the way. When we know that to be true, we know that we have nothing to fear, for He gives us all we need. As we realize God is living life with us, telling His story through us, then we begin to realize the fruits of His spirit are ours.

His power is ours.

His mercy is ours.

His strength is ours.

His persistence is ours.

His deep and unyielding love is ours.

Henry: Fear is often based on a belief that we don't have enough. When we are afraid to tell our story, we question "is it enough?" As we realize that everything God has is ours, we realize we have more than enough.

One of my family's favorite Christmas traditions is making and

decorating Christmas cookies. When it comes to baking, my wife is in charge of the kitchen. About three years ago when we were getting ready to decorate our cookies, my youngest asked, "Mommy how many do we each get to make?"

She was at that age when everybody getting an equal share was really important. So, my wife looked at the bowl of dough and the baking sheets she had laid out and said, "You each get to do a dozen cookies."

The excitement was palatable as Adeline grabbed cookie cutters and Kaitlyn went for the sprinkles. I started rolling out my cookie and used about a quarter of the dough, making one big cookie, almost filling the baking sheet. It was the face of an elf, with its mouth wide open, eating a snake. Really, it was going to be something else completely but when it baked, it morphed into something that kinda resembled that and I decorated away.[6] At this point Adeline got really nervous because my one cookie was bigger than her first ten combined. Although we would each get a dozen cookies, there would be no equity.

This has always been the case in baking. While the gross variations between professional baked goods were not as extreme as my daughters' cookies and mine; bakers quickly noticed they could make more money on less dough. Since the bakers wanted more, they gave people less. Who would really notice if the 4-ounce rolls were really each only 3.9 ounces each?

Because it was so hard to notice, bakers shorting customers became such a big deal that laws were made to prevent it. The severity of the law points to how big of a problem it was. In ancient Egypt, if a baker was found out to be shorting customers they would have their ear nailed to the door of the bakery. In Babylon they would cut the bakers hand clean off. So it is easy to see why the bakers dozen was born.

My mother knew how many a bakers dozen was, but the extra donut she received was a kind hearted gift, overflowing from love.

The bakers dozen didn't get it's start that way though. Those first bakers would steal if they could, but gave only because of fear.

The 13th item could not have been more different, because of the motivation.

> There is no fear in love. But perfect love drives out fear, because fear has to do with punishment. The one who fears is not made perfect in love.[7]

Dani: Our challenge to you has been not to just tell a story, but to live more than a story. Don't do this because you are afraid of what will happen if you don't, but because you are secure in perfect love that frees you to live. When talking about the weight of living into the very depth of your story, it can become terrifying. It's easy to get people to do things - even things as amazing as living more than a story - by scaring them into it, but a life motivated by fear is only half alive. When fear rules our hearts and our minds, there is no room for peace or trust. Fear is like a shadow that casts itself far and wide and takes the radiance away. Fear-based communities cannot support each other, because their own self-acceptance is broken.

In our effort to discover the depth of what makes up our lives, the goal is not to trick people into forced communities because they are afraid they aren't doing it right. This is an invitation to come to the table just as you are and share your story. To be brave and open up about the real things going on in your life with the people around you. To own the hard things and let God work through the conversations that follow. Whether the fear is based in reality or completely irrational, do not let it rule you. Join the community of authentic relationships based in T.R.U.S.T that will hear you, love you, support you, and help you dream outside of the fear.

Henry: What is motivating you matters. At the time when Jesus walked the earth, a Roman soldier could force people to help him carry his gear for a mile. If someone refused, the soldier could fine them, have them arrested, or smack them around a little bit. The

person was motivated by fear and because of this, they counted every step they walked with the soldier. At one mile exactly they would drop what they were carrying and be done. We all have things in our lives that are like that, we just have to do them and can't wait to get them done.

I can't imagine either the solider or the carrier went home with a story to tell. The soldier didn't kiss his wife then tell her how he made another person carry his stuff for a mile. The bag carrier didn't brag about how tough he was. It was in the very midst of this context, Jesus came along and said, "If anyone forces you to go one mile, go with them two miles."[8]

Jesus isn't motivating by fear, like the soldiers.

There is no threat.

Jesus is calling people to happen to the story and create more than a story, even in the midst of their fear. When we freely go the extra mile, we make room for a fruitful harvest like one we've never seen before.

Fifty years ago, my mom received a little something extra. That baker didn't have a plan concocted to inspire my mom to tell me a story so he could end up in a book. But his little action sent ripples that encourage you to be brave, go the extra mile, and to live *more than a story*.

Chapter 1: Theresa's Story

[1] When we allow humans to be nameless, objectification is often the result. Among the most extreme examples of this is the sex trade. "She has a Name" (www.shehasaname.com) *is a movement of Christ followers burdened for victims of human trafficking. Our hope is that God would use us in putting an end to modern-day slavery. Only He can truly set them free and we are excited that He has given us an opportunity to be a part of the solution.*

"She Has A Name" is derived from a real-life story from the streets. There was a "john" (male paying for sex), a pimp and a prostitute. The "john" said to the pimp, "What's her name?" The pimp said, "She doesn't have a name. She is whatever you want her to be."

We try to remember the girls' names when doing street outreach. If we see them again the following week, we'll say their name out loud to them. Their reactions say everything. It's as if they've ached their whole lives to hear their own name. It's as if they forgot their own name. This is why we do street outreach. Even if just for a moment, they believe what we do: that their life matters.

[2] This quote is often misattributed to the 1994 inaugural address by Nelson Mandela, even in the film *Akela and the Bee* (2006, Lions Gate Films), he never said it. Marianne Williamson wrote this quote in *A Return To Love: Reflections on the Principles of A Course in Miracles* (1996, HarperOne).

[3] *Weight of Glory* (2009, HarperOne) is a collection of letters written by C.S. Lewis

[4] The "crowd of witnesses" references Hebrews 12:1-3 says "Therefore, since we are surrounded by such a great cloud of witnesses, let us throw off everything that hinders and the sin that so easily entangles. And let us run with perseverance the race marked out for us, fixing our eyes on Jesus, the pioneer and perfecter of faith. For the joy set before him he endured the cross,

scorning its shame, and sat down at the right hand of the throne of God. Consider him who endured such opposition from sinners, so that you will not grow weary and lose heart.

[5] When most people open the front of a book, it is so easy to skip over the acknowledgements or turn the movie off when the credits role. Unfortunately, so much hard work and other people's efforts go unnoticed. This book wouldn't be the project it is without the great work of so many others who came alongside us. Thank you.

Chapter 2: Frank the Lion Killer

[1] Acts 1:8

[2] If you want to experience another culture, a great place to start is with food, sport, and music. You will be amazed how much you can learn by watching and talking about these three things. Next time you travel, take in one of the local games, eat some indigenous food at a local restaurant, and listen to the street musicians. Exegesis and experience of these things will tell you much of a cultures story.

[3] This language is rare, being used only twice. First Paul (the Apostle, not Dani's husband) writes in Philippians 2:17 "But even if I am being poured out like a drink offering on the sacrifice and service coming from your faith, I am glad and rejoice with all of you." Then in 2 Timothy 4:6 he states "For I am already being poured out like a drink offering, and the time for my departure is near."

Chapter 3: Pea Story

[1] John 1:8

[2] This story is told in Genesis 3:8.

[3] *Love Wins: A book about Heaven, Hell and the Fate of Every Person Who Ever Lived.* (Harper Collins, 2011) Rob Bell

Chapter 4: It's Just My Face

[1] I'm enacting Jay Bakker's footnote in *Faith, Doubt, and Other Lines I've Crossed* (Jericho Books, 2013) where he says, "This is stolen from Peter Rollins. Who knows if it's his or someone else's. I think it's the rule of three: first time you give credit, second time 'I heard it somewhere,' and third time it's 'I was thinking about it.' Preacher's rule. Third time it's yours." However, It was Coach Arnie Ball, not Pete Rollins from whom I'm stealing. Coach Ball taught me T.R.U.S.T years ago, as such the honor of this chapter belongs to him and the error to me.

[2] A very special thanks goes out to Mike and Jennifer and the whole Old Crown crew for all the love, support, table space and sustenance over the years. The beans Ben has roasted have fueled many hours of writing and editing this book. If you are in Fort Wayne, you must stop by 3417 N Anthony Blvd and have the best cup of coffee you've ever tasted... or call them (260) 422-5282 and order a pound - they ship.

[3] Matthew 5:37

[4] *Leading with the Heart: Coach K's Successful Strategies for Basketball, Business, and Life* (Grand Central Publishing, 2010) Mike Krzyzewski

Chapter 5: I Kicked A Dog

[1] Death of the Author, and essay included in *Image, Music, Text* (Hill and Wang, 1978) Roland Barthes addresses this concept elegantly.

[2] For Good (Decca Broadway, 2003) composed by Stephen Schwartz

[3] John 10:10

[4] A huge asterisk belongs by the word "pastor," because I am not an (Ephesians 4:11-13
So Christ himself gave the apostles, the prophets, the evangelists, the pastors and teachers, to equip his people for

works of service, so that the body of Christ may be built up until we all reach unity in the faith and in the knowledge of the Son of God and become mature, attaining to the whole measure of the fullness of Christ.) sense. I believe that the five-fold ministry as unpacked in chapter 10 of Building a Discipleship Culture (3DM, 2011) Mike Breen or what Alan Hirsch calls APEST (www.TheForgottenWays.com/apest) is an essential concept to be rediscovered by the church today.

Chapter 6: The Baby Whisperer

[1] "We cannot love ourselves unless we love others, and we cannot love others unless we love ourselves. But a selfish love of ourselves makes us incapable of loving others. The difficulty of this commandment lies in the paradox that it would have us love ourselves unselfishly, because even our love of ourselves is something we owe to others." Thomas Merton

[2] *Covenant and Kingdom: The DNA of the Bible* (3DM, 2011) Mike Breen

[3] Genesis 22 tells the story of Abraham, a prototypical example of covenant, being asked to kill his first born son Isaac. To many, myself included, this story has never made sense. The headings added in contemporary translations, such as "Abraham Tested," add to the confusion, not only in regard to the story but also into the very essence of God, and peoples relationship with Him.

While I can not recommend Breen's book enough, or better yet attending a 3DM workshop when you can speak with the 3DM team about this (www.weare3dm.com/events) I will grossly summarize here.

The predominant theme of covenant is shared identity. Part of covenantal identity is realizing what's mine is yours and what's yours is mine. Inasmuch, in asking Abraham to sacrifice his son, God was offering His.

[4] John 10:10

[5] Please do not misread this, I am not claiming that this girls father was Satan, any more than Jesus was claiming Peter was Satan in Matthew 16:23. However, it is essential, especially when talking about covenant identity to realize that anything other than the identity that we are baptized into; that is, beloved children of God, is a false identity and a lie (see John 8:44)

[6] Matthew 23:8-10

[7] Matthew 5:11

[8] Matthew 5:14-16

Chapter 7: Machetes and Madmen

We've all been exposed to many thinkers who do not practice and just as many practitioners who do not think. When speaking of repentance as thinking differently after falling into either category would be easy. In 2004, Henry traveled to St.Thomas in Sheffield, England and was exposed to the work of Mike Breen, a true thinking practitioner and practicing thinker. He developed a tool called "the circle," which has helped countless individuals and churches in repenting and belief.

Mike now leads the 3dm team, and as you are digesting the concept of repentance and what to do with it, they are a great resource offering coaching and conferences for individuals and churches. Find out more info at www.3dm.com

We should note Henry is currently coaching for 3dm.

[1] John 19:30 - It is interesting to note that the word Jesus cried out, tetelestai, was a double entendre of sorts. While it is rightly translated as, "it is finished;" the second meaning adds even more depth to the story. This word was written on the bottom of a ledger when a debt was paid off and as such can also be translated as "Paid in Full."

² Psalm 103:12 is a rather paradoxical text in that the distance between the east and the west is either very far or very near, and inasmuch points both to movement and the direction we are heading. That is, if I am walking west the east is eternally far away; yet at the same time it is right behind me.

³ Take a Bow (Def Jam, 2008) Mikkel S. Eriksen, Tor Erik Hermansen, and Shaffer Smith

⁴ As we learn to truly repent, that is "think different after," the voices we invite to the table will have a dramatic effect. Since porn was the example we used, a great voice to invite to the table is XXXchurch.

The resources at www.xxxchurch.com address both men and women. If you are a man, Henry suggests *Every Man's Battle: Every Man's Guide to Winning the War on Sexual Temptation One Victory at a Time* (WaterBrook Press, 2004) Stephen Arterburn and Fred Stoeker which addresses lust and sexuality exclusively. *Wild at Heart: Discovering the Secret of a Man's Soul* (Thomas Nelson, 2001) John Eldredge has some great content that surrounds sexuality and purity but also deals with a lot of other guy stuff. Although, like Wild at Heart, *Fight Club* (www.fightclub414.com) does not deal exclusively with sexuality, they bring some high challenge in this area.

⁵ Some refer to what we call "artistic space" as "prophetic distance." This is based on the APEST / 5-fold ministry that we mentioned footnote 4 of Chapter 5. A base prophet will find creating artistic space natural while other base ministries will struggle with it. If you are not a base prophet, it will be helpful to spend time with one and as Ephesians 4:12 encourages us to "be equipped" and "grow in maturity," in this area.

⁶ Genesis 1:14

⁷ Romans 12:2

⁸ John 13:23, John 19:26, John 21:7 are just a few.

Chapter 8: Shiny Red Blessings

[1] *In Chapter five of Good to Great: Why Some Companies Make the Leap...And Others Don't* (Harper Business,July 19, 2011) Jim Collins the concept of "Level 5 Leadership" is addressed. If you are, in any way, shape, or form, a leader I can not recommend this book more highly. The reality is, Mychal's comment epitomizes this kind of leadership. For a very brief explanations watch http://www.jimcollins.com/media_topics/level-5.html#audio=81

[2] As you read in the previous chapter, we are involved in international mission work. There is an ongoing conversation about how we can do them better and how sometimes are good intentions have caused harm. These two books: *When Helping Hurts: How to Alleviate Poverty Without Hurting the Poor . . .* and *Yourself* (Moody Publishers, 2012) Brian Fikkert, Steve Corbett, John Perkins

and

Toxic Charity: How Churches and Charities Hurt Those They Help (And How to Reverse It) (HarperOne, 2011) Robert D. Lupton are essential reading to entering this conversation.

[3] I listened to Rob Bell's sermons when he was preaching at Mars Hill. While I'm sure this exegesis was not original to him, he introduced to me to this concept.

Chapter 9: Mac and Cheese

[1] How One Lottery Winner Blew Through $10 Million in Less Than 10 Years (2013) Eamon Murphy http://www.dailyfinance.com/2013/03/25/lottery-winner-powerball-sharon-tirabassi/

[2] Luke 4:36-37

[3] We don't want to minimize resource management, especially financial stewardship. Dave Ramsey has a great 9 week course called *Financial Peace* (http://www.daveramsey.com/fpu) and has written numerous books *The Total Money Makeover: A Proven*

Plan for Financial Fitness (Thomas Nelson, 2003) Dave Ramsey is my personal favorite.

[4] In Matthew 7:13-14 Jesus speaks of the small gate and narrow. While Jesus himself claims to be the both the road and the gate; the question I find myself asking is how do I live on this road in the here and now. The early church found the answer paradoxically, in the very embracing (or refusing to embrace) both sides. This is what Paul speaks of in Galatians 3:28. Peter Rollins exegesis (http://peterrollins.net/2010/11/i-do-not-bring-peace-but-a-sword/) on this text, like much of his work is worth the read and will provoke thoughts and conversations.

[5] After a bit of overspending one Christmas, a couple decided to forgo shopping for the month, with the exception of a gallon of milk each week. It turned out that they were able to live off of only the food in their cupboards not only for the month but over 6 weeks.

[6] *Reach out in Love: Stories Told by Mother Teresa* Compiled and Edited by Edward Le Joly and Jaya Chaliha

[7] Matthew 25:31-46

[8] Although this quote is not in the film, you order the The Shadow of Virtue exclusively from Humdinger Pictures ttp://www.humdingerpictures.com/shadows_of_virtue.html

[9] While these five parts of a story are outlined in a grade school text, in *A Million Miles in a Thousand Years: What I Learned While Editing My Life* (Thomas Nelson , 2009) Donald Miller unpacks and applies them wonderfully.

[10] Matthew 10:39

[11] James 1:27

Chapter 10: What a Twister Stirs Up

[1] Matthew 10:12

[2] When Jesus sends out the 12 in Matthew 10:1-20, and then the 72 in Luke 10:1-16, He tells them to look for people who: welcome them, listen to them, and serve them. The shorthand for these people is "Person of Peace." My friend Ben Sternke blogs about this http://bensternke.com/2011/11/the-key-to-recognizing-a-person-of-peace/

[3] Although she doesn't use the term "social kindness" in chapter 8 of *Communication in Our Lives* (Wadsworth Publishing, 2013) Julia T. Wood explores this issue in her discussion of levels of confirmation and disconfirmation.

[4] To those who are people of peace, Jesus says "move in" (Luke 10:7 and Matthew 10:11) but to those who are not Jesus says "move on" (Luke 10:10-11 and Matthew 10:14).

Chapter 11: I Wanted To Get You Flowers, So…

[1] *The Five Love Languages: The Secret to Love that Lasts* (Northfield Publishing, 2009) Gary Chapman. This book is the base for how Paul and I approach our marriage and it has been an incredibly helpful tool. I highly recommend it for all types of relationships.

[2] *Becoming Human* (Paulist Pr, 2008) Jean Vanier

[3] Although many of Jesus parables tell what the kingdom is, only in Mark 1:15 does He tell how it breaks in. The word that we translate "time," is not chronological time (chronos) but a moment (kairos). As we recognize moment, repent and act on our new thoughts (that is what believe means) the kingdom of heaven breaks in.

As I've coached people in recognizing kairos, many work under the false assumption that if it is not "big" it can't be a kairos. One man shared a kairos that his wife had packed his bag and left them on the front porch with a note that basically said "move out." While this is a kairos, I'd classify it as a "brick wall" kairos. There are really four types of kairos that I have observed and while the "brick wall" is one, there are usually many "speed bumps" that lead up to it. Recognizing "speed bump" kairos is very helpful and less painful. In the case of my friend you can imagine the speed bumps leading up to "brick wall."

Another type of kairos individuals usually have are "crystal ball" moments. In these an individual realizes, for better or worse, it could be like that. For example, when my friend had his "brick wall" kairos moment, Tricia and I were arguing a lot and I though if something doesn't changes that could be us. Since I've used two negative examples, I should mention kairos can also be positive. When I was a youth director, I saw a great youth group where the students were growing in their faith and I though, "We could be like that." Much like a "crystal ball" kairos, the fourth type is the "mirror." In this type rather than thinking "I could be like that," one realized "I am like that."

I am not claiming this is an exhaustive list of types of kairos moment, but I have found these categories are helpful to those struggling to see kairos in their lives.

Chapter 12: Candles, Cake, Cocaine

[1] While contemporary Americans tend to focus on the nuclear family, this is a historic anomaly. In *The Way We Never Were: American Families And The Nostalgia Trap* (Basic Books, 1992) Stephanie Coontz explores this other myths around the American family.

The word oikos in the bible is what we translate "family" or "household." It extended not only beyond mom, dad and 2.4 kids to cousins, uncles, aunts and grandparents but also beyond blood relations. Household servants and other non-blood relations wer part of the oikos.

[2] Promise Minsistries has services during the school year at 9:00am and 10:30am. Junior Worship occurs for children during the

10:30 service. We are located at 7323 Schwartz Rd. Fort Wayne, Indiana 46815 Services times do change during the summer because of our Camp Promise (www.CampPromiseFW.com) so call (260)493-9953 or check our website (www.PromiseMInistries.org) for service times.

[3] Ephesians 2:8-9

[4] *The Ragamuffin Gospel: Good News for the Bedraggled, Beat-Up, and Burnt Out* (Multnomah Books, 2008) Brennan Manning

[5] You can find out more about Saint Nicolas at http://en.wikipedia.org/wiki/Saint_Nicholas My favorite tale is when he was debating Arius during the counsel of Nicaea, and punched him (http://www.stnicholascenter.org/pages/bishop-nicholas-loses-his-cool/). This is one tale rarely told about Santa on Christmas Eve.

[6] Romans 6:23

[7] Ephesians 2:4

[8] Ephesians 2:8-9

[9] Ephesians 2:10

[10] *Daring Greatly: How the Courage to Be Vulnerable Transforms the Way We Live, Love, Parent, and Lead* (Gotham Books, 2012) Brene Brown

Chapter 13: Baker's Dozen

[1] This is a concept drawn from proxemics: Intimate space is 1-2 other people, Personal space is groups of 4-12, Social Space consists of groups of 13-120, and public space is over 120. People function differently in each of these spaces. In *Launching Missional Communities: A Field Guide* (3DM, 2010) Mike Breen and Alex Absalom explore the fact that each of the larger spaces are made up of smaller spaces . That is, public space has several groups of social space within it. This is why if a dinner gets bigger than 13 it from Personal Space into Social Space there will be at least

two conversations going on. This is why I always try to sit in the middle, because as an extrovert I want to be in both conversations.

In Chapter 5 of *The Tipping Point: How Little Things Can Make a Big Difference* (Little, Brown and Company, 2006) Malcom Gladwell explores the practicals of how public space function, although he never uses the term. After reading it and watching churches go mega, I believe there is a particular function of mega space that has yet to be researched. The only thing I remember from my intro to psychological statistics course at University of North Texas was that every good paper should say "Further research is needed in this area." While I believe this to be true I have neither the time nor the desire to explore this theory; However this would make a great graduate thesis and I would gladly consult. I'm sure I put my cell phone number in this book somewhere

[2] The Club with More U.S. Presidents than Skull and Bones (December 14, 2011 - 7:23pm) Mental_Floss http://mentalfloss. com/article/29502/club-more-us-presidents-skull-and-bones

[3] Teddy Roosevelt and FDR were fifth cousins; however, Eleanor (FDR's wife) was Elliot's (Teddy's brother) daughter making her his niece. http://www.funtrivia.com/askft/Question41379.html

[4] Excerpt from the speech "Citizenship In A Republic" delivered by Theodore Roosevelt at the Sorbonne, in Paris, France on 23 April, 1910

[5] Joshua 1:9

[6] If you want to see Henry's Christmas cookies just check out his twitter feed @henrygraf - the cookie I describe above was tweeted on 17 December 2011

[7] 1 John 4:18

[8] Matthew 5:41

Dani Tietjen coauthored *More Than A Story*. She is a nationally sought after public speaker who shares her ministry and life through her blog (**www. DaniTietjen.com**) which has an international following. She is a philanthropist and humanitarian on a team of dedicated people who founded the Haiti Mission Project. Dani lives in north Minneapolis with her husband Paul and three children: Noah, Caleb, and Lu.

Henry Graf coauthored *More Than a Story*. He is the Pastor of Promise LCMS in Fort Wayne, Indiana and coaches for 3DM. He holds both a Master of Divinity and a Master of Art in Communication. You can follow his blog (**www.HenryGraf.com**) to keep up with his latest thoughts, devotions, and projects. Henry is married to his beloved Tricia and they have two daughters: Kaitlyn and Adeline.